The Official
Driver Theory Test
Cars, Motorcycles and
Works vehicles
Questions and Answers

Published by Prometric Ireland Limited under licence from the Road Safety Authority.

© 2017 Údarás Um Shábháilteacht Ar Bhóithre / Road Safety Authority

June 2017 Edition

ISBN 9780995513082

Prometric
La Touche House
Custom House Dock
IFSC
Dublin 1
DO1 R5P3
IRELAND

Foreword

As a learner driver, it is important that you have all the information you need to drive safely and in a socially responsible way on our roads. Before you drive on a public road or in a public place you must have a learner permit or a driving licence for the vehicle you want to drive. In most cases you must also pass a driver theory test to show that you understand what you must do to drive safely. The questions in the car, tractor, work vehicle,motorcycle and moped driver theory tests, which are all in this book, are designed to test your knowledge and also to make you think about the different situations you will come across as a driver. By studying the learning material and passing the test you will have taken an important first step to becoming a safe driver. It is essential that you then apply your knowledge when you are on the road.

Learning to drive needs time and patience, and the best way to learn is to take driving lessons while practising as much as you can with an experienced driver. Learners taking out a first learner permit for a car must take the Essential Driver Training (EDT) programme, and learners taking out a learner permit for a motorcycle must take Initial Basic Training (IBT) – for more information, see www.rsa.ie. It is important to find an Approved Driving Instructor (ADI) that you are comfortable with and to listen carefully to the advice you get. Ask for help if you aren't sure of something and look up your copy of the Rules of the Road for guidance.

Finally, remember that driving should be enjoyable, and we wish you many years of safe driving.

Introduction and how to obtain a driving licence

Section 1: All vehicle categories

Section 2: Cars, Light Vans, Tractors and Works Vehicles

Section 3: Motorcycles and mopeds

Introduction

To drive a motor vehicle on the public road in Ireland, you must hold a driving licence or a learner permit that covers the particular category of vehicle you plan to drive. For licensing purposes, there are fourteen categories of vehicle, identified by code letters – for example a motorcar is category B, a moped is category AM.

With a learner permit, a number of restrictions apply, the most important of which is that for most types of vehicle you must be accompanied at all times by the holder of a full driving licence in the category of vehicle you are driving.

Changes to the Driver Theory Test

From 1st June 2017 any person applying to sit the Driver Theory Test will be asked to confirm they have a Public Services Card and will be required to present it at the test centre as proof of ID. At the time of booking the test, applicants will be asked to confirm that they possess a Public Services Card.

If you don't yet have a Public Services Card you can make an appointment to get one either by using MyWelfare.ie or by calling into your local Intreo Centre (local social welfare office.) Any queries about this application process should be made by telephone on 1890 927 999 or 01 7043281.

Who must take the driver theory test?

Before you can apply for your first learner permit in any driving licence category, you must have passed a driver theory test that relates to that category, and you must submit the driver theory test certificate to the licensing authority within two years of passing the test.

There are four different driver theory tests; which one you take depends on the category of vehicle you are planning to drive. This book covers all questions for the Car, Motorcycle, Works vehicles and Tractor driver theory tests, and different parts of the book are relevant to different tests, as shown below.

Category of vehicle you intend to drive		Parts of this book you need to study for driver theory test
B	Car and light van BW	Parts 1 and 2
BE	Car and light van with trailer	Parts 1 and 2
W	Tractor and works vehicle	Parts 1 and 2
A	Motorcycle	Parts 1 and 3
A1	Small motorcycle	Parts 1 and 3
A2	Restricted motorcycle	Parts 1 and 3
AM	Moped	Parts 1 and 3

Note that you do not have to pass the same theory test more than once. For example, if you pass the theory test for category B and obtain a learner permit for category B, and you subsequently wish to obtain a learner permit for category BE, you are not required to take another driver theory test, provided you still have a valid learner permit or driving licence for category B.

Preparing for the driver theory test

You should use this book, and/or the Driver Theory Test CD-ROM as well as the Rules of the Road to prepare for the driver theory test. This book contains the actual questions that will be asked in your Car Motorcycle Tractor and driver theory tests, along with the correct answer and a brief explanation. All of the questions and learning materials contained in this book along with practice exams are also available via the online learning service at https://dttstore.prometric.com/

If you spend sufficient time and effort preparing for your test, you should not find it difficult, and you should pass. More importantly, the knowledge you gain in preparing for the test will help to make you a better and a safer driver.

About the questions and answers in this book

In this book, you are presented with a question, the correct answer and an explanation as to why the answer is correct. Some questions may show a graphic which requires interpretation. For example:

What does this sign mean?

Stop your vehicle.

ABMW0001

This sign appears at junctions where a minor road joins a major road. You must stop your vehicle completely at a STOP sign.

In the test, you will be asked 40 questions, and to pass you must answer at least 35 correctly. The questions will be taken from those set out in this book – you will not get a question that is not in the book.

In the test, each question you are asked is accompanied by four possible answers. Only one of these answers is correct, and you are required to identify it. The test is computerised and you will get a chance to practice before the test, so that you are familiar with the format.

Note: Some graphics are used on on more than one question but the scenario is different.

Applying for a driver theory test

When you feel that you are well-enough prepared, apply to the Official Driver Theory Testing Service in one of the following ways:

Online:	www.theorytest.ie.
By telephone:	For an English language test call: 1890 606 106 For an Irish language test call: 1890 606 806 (These telephone numbers are all LoCall numbers.)
By post:	Complete an application form (obtainable from any National Driver Licence Service (NDLS) centre or online from: www.theorytest.ie) and post it to: The Driver Theory Testing Service, PO Box 15, Dundalk, Co. Louth When applying, please specify any special needs or language requirements that you have, so that appropriate arrangements may be made.

When booking a test, please have to hand credit/debit card details and your PPS number (formally RSI number).

Information on where and when theory tests may be taken can be obtained by contacting the Driver Theory Testing Service as above.

How to Obtain a Category B Driving Licence (Car)

Test Preparation

- Study The Official Driver Theory Test (DTT) Question & Answers Book or The Official Driver Theory Test CD-ROM. Available to purchase at **www.theorytest.ie** and also at major book stores in Ireland.

- Some Approved Driving Instructors (ADIs) help prepare learners for their Driver Theory Test.

Theory Test

- Book Category B Theory Test online via **www.theorytest.ie** or by telephoning **1890 606 106**

- Sit & pass Theory Test

- Obtain DTT Certificate

Learner Permit

- Apply for Category B Learner Permit at any National Driver Licence Service (NDLS) Public Office See **www.ndls.ie**

ADI & Sponsor

- Study the learning to drive process. Get to know what you should expect and what if any preparatory work you need to do ahead of your first formal driving lesson.

- Choose an ADI and a Sponsor so you can begin the process of learning to drive. Scan here to watch this video on the role of a Sponsor:

Practical Driving Test

- Once your ADI advises you to, you should book your Practical Driving Test via **www.drivingtest.ie**.

Note: It will not be possible to sit your test until the RSA have received confirmation that your EDT has been completed

- Sit and pass Practical Driving Test. Scan here to watch this video on the Day of the driving test

- Obtain Certificate of Competency

EDT

- In addition to the standard formal driving lessons, learners are now required to complete the Essential Driver training (EDT programme)

- When advised you are ready, complete each of the 12 hours EDT with an RSA registered Advanced Driver Instructor (ADI). Your ADI will let you know when you are ready for your next EDT lesson. Scan here to watch a video on Essential Driver Training

- Complete planned practice sessions with your Sponsor

- Ensure Official Log Book is completed

- Visit 'MY EDT' on RSA website to ensure all your EDT lessons records have been uploaded

Note: Be guided by your ADI on when to practice your driving and what to practice.

Driving Licence

- Apply for Category B Driving Licence at any National Driver Licence Service (NDLS) Public Office. See **www.ndls.ie**.

- Obtain Category B Driving Licence.

IMPORTANT

Continue to practice what you have learned. Drive in a safe and socially responsible manner to keep you, your family and friends as well as other road users safe.

How to Obtain a Category A Driving Licence (Motorcycle)

Test Preparation

- Study The Official Driver Theory Test Question & Answers Book or The Official Driver Theory Test CD-ROM. Available to purchase at **www.theorytest.ie** and also at major book stores in Ireland.

- Some Approved Driving Instructors (ADIs) help prepare learners for their Driver Theory Test.

Theory Test

- Book Category AM Theory Test online via **www.theorytest.ie** or by telephoning **1890 606 106**

- Sit & pass Theory Test

- Obtain DTT Certificate

ADI

- Choose an Approved Driving Instructor (ADI) so you can begin the process of Initial Basic Training (IBT). IBT is a mandatory training course that teaches basic riding skills to learner motorcyclists.

Learner Permit

- Apply for relevant Motorcycle category learner permit at any National Driver Licence Service (NDLS) Public Office. See **www.ndls.ie**.

- Read the Initial Basic Training (IBT) information book.

Practical Driving Test

- Book Practical Driving Test via **www.drivingtest.ie**.

Note: It will not be possible to sit your test until the RSA have received confirmation that your IBT has been completed.

- Sit and pass Practical Driving Test

- Obtain Certificate of Competency

- Scan to watch this video on the day of your practical driving test

- Obtain Certificate of Competency

IBT

- Complete at least 16 hours of Initial Basic Training (IBT) with an RSA registered Advanced Driver Instructor (ADI).

- Ensure Official Log Book is completed

- Be guided by your instructor as to when you should apply for your practical driving test

- Obtain Certification of Satisfactory Completion

Driving Licence

- Apply for relevant Motorcycle category Driving Licence at any National Driver Licence Service (NDLS) Public Offices. See **www.ndls.ie**.

- Obtain relevant category of Motorcycle Driving Licence.

IMPORTANT

Continue to practice what you have learned. Ride your motorcycle in a safe and socially responsible manner to keep you and other road users safe.

Road signs, markings and traffic regulations

As you drive along any road you are receiving information all the time, and you need to be able to take in this information and respond as necessary. Much of the information that you need to understand comes from regulatory road signs and markings that tell you things that you must do.

The questions in this section are designed to check that you know:

The meaning of all the road signs and markings that you might meet when you are driving:

- Regulatory signs and markings that tell you things you must do;
- Signs that give you advance warning of when you should take special care; and
- Motorway signs;

The regulations relating to speed;

The regulations relating to parking; and

The meaning of the various hand signals that a garda might make, and the hand signals you might need to make yourself.

Regulatory traffic signs

Regulatory traffic signs are those that you must obey. Most of them are circular in shape, have a red border and symbols or text in black. The STOP and YIELD signs have unique shapes so that they cannot be confused with any other signs.

What does this sign mean?
ABMW0001

Stop your vehicle.

This sign appears at junctions where a minor road joins a major road. You must stop your vehicle completely at a STOP sign.

What must a driver do when this sign is accompanied by a white stop line on the road?
ABMW0002R

Stop at the line.

When accompanied by a STOP sign, the white stop line indicates the point at which you must stop your vehicle.

What must a driver do when this sign is NOT accompanied by a white stop line on the road?
ABMW0003R

Stop at the sign.

Where a STOP sign is not accompanied by a white stop line, you must stop at the sign.

What does this sign mean at a junction?
ABMW0004R

Yield to traffic on the major road.

At a junction, the YIELD sign tells you that you must give way to traffic on a major road ahead. This means that you must slow down and be prepared to stop.

What does this sign mean at a roundabout?
ABMW0005R

Yield to traffic coming from the right.

At a roundabout, the YIELD sign tells you that you must slow down and be prepared to stop. You must yield (give way) to traffic already on the roundabout.

1
2
3

What does this sign mean?

ABMW0006R

Straight ahead only.

This sign tells you that you must proceed straight ahead. It is usually displayed on the entry to a one-way street.

What does this sign mean?

ABMW0007

Turn left only.

This sign tells you that you must turn left. It is usually displayed at a junction where all traffic must turn left – for example, in a one-way system that incorporates a junction.

What does this sign mean?

ABMW0008

Turn right only.

This sign tells you that you must turn right. It is usually displayed at a junction where all traffic must turn right – for example, in a one-way system that incorporates a junction.

What does this sign mean?

ABMW0009R

Turn left ahead.

This sign tells you that you must turn left ahead. It is usually displayed on the approach to a one-way system.

What does this sign mean?

ABMW0010

Turn right ahead.

This sign tells you that you must turn right ahead. It is usually displayed on the approach to a one-way system.

What does this sign mean?

ABMW0011R

Keep left.

This sign tells you that you must keep left. It is usually displayed at a traffic island in the centre of the road.

1
2
3

What does this sign mean?
ABMW0012R

Keep right.

This sign tells you that you must keep right. It is usually found in a one-way system where the traffic is required to keep to the right.

What does this sign mean?
ABMW0013

Pass either side.

This sign tells you that traffic must pass on either side of the traffic island.

What does this sign mean?
ABMW0014R

No entry.

This sign tells you that you must not proceed in the direction of the arrow. This is displayed to prevent traffic going in the wrong direction – for example, the wrong way up a one-way street.

What does this sign mean?
ABMW0015R

No right turn.

This sign is displayed at a junction where you may not turn right.

What does this sign mean?
ABMW0017R

No left turn.

This sign is displayed at a junction where you may not turn left.

What does this sign mean?
ABMW0018R

U-turn not permitted.

This sign tells you that you are not permitted to make a U-turn. It is displayed at junctions on dual carriageways. U-turns are also not permitted anywhere there is a continuous white line along the centre of the road or on a one-way street.

1
2
3

What does this sign mean?
ABMW0019

Maximum speed is 30km/h.

This sign tells you that the maximum legal speed limit permitted for this section of road is 30km/h.

What does this sign mean?
ABMW0020

Maximum speed is 50km/h.

This sign tells you that the maximum legal speed limit permitted for this section of road is 50km/h.

What does this sign mean?
ABMW0021

Maximum speed is 60km/h.

This sign tells you that the maximum legal speed limit permitted for this section of road is 60km/h.

What does this sign mean?
ABMW0022R

Maximum speed is 80km/h.

This sign tells you that the maximum legal speed limit permitted for this section of road is 80km/h.

What does this sign mean?
ABMW0023

Maximum speed is 100km/h.

This sign tells you that the maximum legal speed limit permitted for this section of road is 100km/h.

What does this sign mean?
ABMW0024

Maximum speed is 120km/h.

This sign tells you that the maximum legal speed limit permitted for this section of road is 120km/h.

1
2
3

What do these signs together mean?
ABMW0025

Parking permitted at times shown.

These signs tells you that parking is permitted in both directions, but only at the times shown on the information plate.

What does this sign mean?
ABMW0026

Parking prohibited.

This sign tells you that parking is prohibited in both directions.

What do these signs together mean?
ABMW0027

Clearway – no stopping or parking during the times shown.

A Clearway sign means that no stopping or parking is allowed in this area during the times shown on the information plate.

What does this sign mean?
ABMW0028

Disc parking operates during the time shown.

This sign tells you your vehicle must display a parking disc when you park during the hours shown on the information plate.

What does this sign mean?
ABMW0029R

Appointed rank for taxis.

A Taxi Rank sign indicates that this is an area reserved for taxis, and parking is not permitted there.

What do these signs together mean?
ABMW0030

Start of cycle track.

This sign indicates the start of a cycle track. If the track is bounded by a broken white line, other road users should avoid using it wherever possible. If it is bounded by a continuous white line, drivers of cars and other vehicles must not drive on it.

What does this sign mean?
ABMW0031

Shared cycle/pedestrian track.

This sign indicates the start of a cycle and pedestrian track. If the track is bounded by a broken white line, other road users should avoid using it wherever possible. If it is bounded by a continuous white line, drivers of cars and other vehicles must not drive on it.

What does this sign mean?
ABMW0032R

Stop for school warden.

This sign is used by a school warden. When the warden raises this sign, you must stop and wait until the schoolchildren have crossed the road.

What do these signs together mean?
ABMW0033R

Pedestrianised street ahead – traffic not allowed except during times shown.

This sign tells you that there is a pedestrian area ahead and that traffic is not allowed except during the times stated on the information plate.

What does this sign mean?
ABMW0034

Maximum permitted weight is 3 tonnes.

This sign tells you that that you must not enter this area if your vehicle is over the stated weight limit.

What does this sign mean?
ABMW0038

Parking of vehicles exceeding the weight shown is not allowed.

This sign tells you that you must not park in this area if your vehicle is over the weight limit indicated.

What does this sign mean?
ABMW0039

No overtaking

This sign tells you that overtaking is prohibited in this area because it is dangerous to do so.

What do these signs together mean?
ABMW0040R

Only buses, cyclists and taxis are allowed to use the lane during the hours indicated.

This sign tells you there is a with-flow bus lane ahead – that is, one where the buses move in the same direction as the traffic to their right.

The information plate tells the times when the bus lane is in operation. Only buses, taxis and cyclists may use the bus lane during those hours.

What does this sign mean?
ABMW0041R

'With flow' bus and cycle lane ahead on left.

This sign tells you there is a with-flow bus lane ahead to the left. Only buses, taxis and cyclists may use the bus lane during the stated operational hours.

1
2
3

23

What does this sign mean?
ABMW0042R

'With flow' bus and cycle lane on left.

This sign indicates a with-flow bus lane ahead. Only buses, taxis and cyclists may use the bus lane during the stated operational hours.

What does this sign mean?
ABMW0043R

Bus and cycle lane ahead on right.

This sign tells you that there is a bus lane ahead to the right. Only buses, taxis and cyclists may use the bus lane during the stated operational hours.

What does this sign mean?
ABMW0045R

'Contra flow' bus lane ahead.

This sign tells you that you must drive on the left and not use the contra-flow bus lane ahead day or night. A contra-flow bus lane is one where the buses are going in the opposite direction to the traffic on their right.

What does this sign mean?
ABMW2

Tram lane on left.

This sign tells you there is a tram lane on the left. Be aware that there might be pedestrians in the area and crossing the road.

Warning signs

Warning signs give you advance notice of changes in the road layout, of junctions and bends ahead, and of anything that might cause a hazard. Most warning signs are diamond shaped with black symbols on a yellow background.

You don't have to do anything when you see a warning sign, but in many cases you will need to make some change in your driving. For example, you might need to slow down as you approach a sharp bend or when you know there is a school ahead.

What does this sign mean?
ABMW0051R

Junction ahead with roads of lesser importance.

This sign gives advance warning of a junction ahead with minor roads on either side. Be aware that vehicles may be emerging from the minor roads.

What does this sign mean?
ABMW0052R

Main road bears to the left.

This sign gives advance warning of a junction with a minor road ahead. The wider arm of the Y indicates the course of the main road.

What does this sign mean?
ABMW0053R

Staggered crossroads ahead with roads of equal importance.

This sign gives advance warning of a staggered junction ahead with roads to the left and right. Be aware that vehicles may be emerging from these roads.

What does this sign mean?
ABMW0054R

Crossroads ahead with roads of equal importance.

This sign gives advance warning of a junction with roads of equal importance ahead. At this type of junction you should yield to traffic approaching from the right and traffic already turning.

1
2
3

What does this sign mean?

ABMW0055R

T-junction ahead with road of equal importance.

This sign gives advance warning of a T-junction ahead with a road of equal importance. You must give way to traffic already on the road you are joining.

What does this sign mean?

ABMW0056R

Y-junction ahead with roads of equal importance.

This sign gives advance warning of a Y-junction ahead with roads of equal importance. Approach such a junction with caution and be prepared to react to any changes in the traffic situation.

What does this sign mean?

ABMW0058R

Major road ahead.

This sign gives advance warning of a crossroads junction with a major road ahead. Be prepared to stop.

What does this sign mean?

ABMW0059R

T-junction ahead with a road of major importance.

This sign gives advance warning of a T-junction with a major road ahead. Be prepared to stop.

What does this sign mean?

ABMW0060R

Crossroads with dual carriageway ahead.

This sign gives advance warning of a crossroads junction with a dual carriageway ahead. Be prepared to stop and give way to other traffic.

What does this sign mean?

ABMW0061R

T-junction with dual carriageway ahead.

This sign gives advance warning of a T-junction with a dual carriageway ahead. Be prepared to stop and give way to other traffic.

What does this sign mean?
Traffic merging from the left.

ABMW0062R

This sign gives advance warning of traffic merging from the left ahead. You should expect vehicles to join from the left ahead and you may need to slow down to allow them to merge.

What does this sign mean?
Traffic merging/diverging ahead.

ABMW0063R

This sign gives advance warning of roads merging and diverging at the left ahead. You should be prepared for traffic changing direction ahead as vehicles may be entering or exiting at the junctions on the left.

What does this sign mean?
Roundabout ahead.

ABMW0064R

This sign gives advance warning of a roundabout ahead. You must prepare to yield to vehicles already on the roundabout coming from the right.

What does this sign mean?
Mini-roundabout ahead.

ABMW0065R

This sign gives advance warning of a mini-roundabout ahead. You must prepare to yield to vehicles already on the roundabout coming from the right.

What does this sign mean?
Dangerous corner ahead.

ABMW0066

This sign gives advance warning of a dangerous corner to the left. You should slow down and be prepared to react to any changes in the traffic situation.

What does this sign mean?
Dangerous bend ahead.

ABMW0067

This sign gives advance warning of a dangerous bend ahead. You should slow down and be prepared to react to any changes in the traffic situation.

1
2
3

What does this sign mean?

ABMW0068

Series of dangerous corners ahead.

This sign gives advance warning of a series of dangerous corners ahead. You should slow down and be prepared to react to any changes in the traffic situation.

What does this sign mean?

ABMW0069R

Series of dangerous bends ahead.

This sign gives advance warning of a series of dangerous bends ahead. You should slow down and be prepared to react to any changes in the traffic situation.

What does this sign mean?

ABMW0070R

Sharp change of direction to the right.

This sign gives advance warning of a sharp change of direction to the right. You should slow down as you approach the hazard.

What does this sign mean?

ABMW0071R

Road narrows on the left.

This sign gives advance warning that the road narrows on the left ahead. You should show caution and prepare to move to the right.

What does this sign mean?

ABMW0072

Road narrows on both sides.

This sign gives advance warning that the road is narrowing ahead. You should show caution and prepare to slow down.

What does this sign mean?

ABMW0073R

Road divides ahead.

This sign gives advance warning that the road divides ahead. You should prepare to move to the left.

What does this sign mean?
ABMW0074

Dual carriageway ends.

This sign gives advance warning of the end of a dual carriageway. You will soon be entering a 2-way road.

What does this sign mean?
ABMW0075

Two-way traffic ahead.

This sign gives advance warning of two-way traffic ahead, with oncoming traffic in the opposite lane.

What does this sign mean?
ABMW0076

Sharp descent ahead.

This sign gives advance warning of a steep downward slope ahead. You should react accordingly by adjusting speed and selecting the appropriate gear.

What does this sign mean?
ABMW0077

Sharp ascent ahead.

This sign gives advance warning of a steep upward hill ahead . You should react by selecting the appropriate gear.

What does this sign mean?
ABMW0078

Restricted headroom up ahead.

This sign gives advance warning that you are approaching an area of restricted headroom, such as a low bridge.

What does this sign mean?
ABMW0079

Overhead electric cables.

This sign gives advance warning of electric cables overhead. Drivers with a high load should be particularly careful.

1
2
3

What does this sign mean?
ABMW0080R

Level crossing ahead unguarded by gates or barriers.

This sign gives advanced warning of an unguarded level crossing ahead. This is a crossing without gates or barriers and you should cross it with extreme caution.

What does this sign mean?
ABMW0081

Level crossing ahead guarded by gates or barriers.

This sign gives advance warning of a railway crossing ahead that is protected by gates or lifting barriers. You should be prepared to stop and follow the required procedure.

What does this sign mean?
ABMW0082

Level crossing ahead with lights and barriers.

This sign gives advance warning of a railway level crossing ahead with lights and barriers . You should be prepared to stop.

STOP
nuair a lasann na soilse dearga

STOP When Red Lights Show

What does this sign mean?
ABMW0083

The driver must stop when red lights show.

This sign gives advance warning that you must stop when red lights show. This sign may be displayed at a railway level crossing.

GO MALL
Crosaire Comhréidh Uathoibríoch

SLOW Automatic Level Crossing

What does this sign mean?
ABMW0084R

Automatic level crossing ahead.

This sign gives advance warning of automatic level crossing ahead. Prepare to stop.

What does this sign mean?
ABMW0085R

Sharp rise in the road ahead – for example, a humpback bridge.

This sign gives advance warning of a hump in the road. You should adjust your speed accordingly.

What does this sign mean?
ABMW0086R

Sharp depression or dip ahead.

This sign gives advance warning of a dip or depression in the road ahead. You should reduce your speed accordingly.

What does this sign mean?
ABMW0087R

Series of bumps or hollows ahead.

This sign gives advance warning of a series of bumps or hollows ahead. You should reduce your speed accordingly.

What does this sign mean?
ABMW0088

Slippery stretch of road ahead.

This sign gives advance warning that there might be a danger of skidding because of an uncertain road surface ahead.

What does this sign mean?
ABMW0089R

Unprotected quay, canal or river ahead.

This sign gives advance warning of an open water area ahead. You should show caution in this situation.

What does this sign mean?
ABMW0090R

Traffic signals ahead.

This sign gives advance warning of a traffic light controlled junction ahead where drivers might not see the lights in good time – for example, following a bend in the road.

What does this sign mean?
ABMW0091R

School ahead.

This sign gives advance warning of a school ahead. You should adjust your speed accordingly as there may be children in the area.

1
2
3

What does this sign mean?
ABMW0092

School children crossing ahead.

This sign gives advance warning that there may be school children crossing the road ahead, and you should be prepared to stop.

What do these signs together mean?
ABMW0094

Beware of children crossing.

These signs are usually displayed in residential areas, and they give advance warning that children might be crossing ahead. You should drive with extra caution.

What does this sign mean?
ABMW0095R

Accompanied horses and ponies ahead.

This sign gives advance warning that there may be horses on the road ahead. You should show due regard for horses and their riders.

What does this sign mean?
ABMW0096

Possibility of cattle or farm animals ahead.

This sign gives advance warning that there may be cattle or other farm animals on the road ahead.

What does this sign mean?
ABMW0097

Possibility of sheep ahead.

This sign gives advance warning that there may be sheep on the road ahead.

What does this sign mean?
Possibility of deer or wild animals ahead.

ABMW0098

This sign gives advance warning that there may be deer or other wild animals coming onto the roadway.

What does this sign mean?
Crosswinds.

ABMW0099R

This sign gives advance warning that there may be crosswinds ahead. Crosswinds can affect the stability of your vehicle on the road.

What does this sign mean?
Pedestrian crossing ahead.

ABMW00100R

This sign gives advance warning of a pedestrian crossing ahead. You should show caution and be prepared to stop.

What does this sign mean?
Tunnel ahead.

ABMW00101R

This sign gives advance warning of a tunnel ahead. You should be aware of the procedures to follow when entering a tunnel – such as turning on headlights.

What does this sign mean?
Danger of falling rocks ahead.

ABMW0102R

This sign gives advance warning that there is a danger of rocks and other debris falling onto the road.

1
2
3

What does this sign mean?

ABMW0103R

Possibility of low flying aircraft.

This sign gives advance warning that there may be low-flying aircraft in the area. Low-flying aircraft can make a loud noise.

What does this sign mean?

ABMW0104R

A driver must drive on the left-hand side.

This sign is generally in areas where tourists might be travelling and reminds motorists to drive on the left.

What does this sign mean?

ABMW0105R

Tramway crossing ahead.

This sign gives advance warning of a tram crossing ahead. You should be prepared to stop and yield to the tram, if required.

What does this sign mean?

ABMW0106R

Tramway crossing ahead.

This sign gives pedestrians advance warning of a tram crossing where they should look both ways before crossing the road.

Motorway signs

Driving on a motorway presents a different set of challenges. In general, traffic is moving faster than on national or regional roads, and you need to plan your journey more carefully in advance.

Only drivers with a full licence may drive on a motorway.

What does this sign mean?
ABMW0109R

Entry to motorway.

This is a motorway information sign telling you that you are entering a motorway.

What does this sign mean?
ABMW0110

Motorway ends 500 metres ahead.

This is a motorway information sign that tells you that the motorway will end in 500 metres.

What does this sign mean?
ABMW0111R

End of motorway.

This sign indicates the end of the motorway. You are now leaving the motorway and its restrictions no longer apply.

What does this sign mean?
ABMW0112R

Three hundred meters to the next exit.

This is a motorway information sign that tells you that the next exit off the motorway is 300 metres ahead.

What does this sign mean?
ABMW0113R

200 metres to the next exit.

This is a motorway information sign that tells you that the next exit off the motorway is 200 metres ahead.

1
2
3

What does this sign mean?

ABMW0114R

100 metres to the next exit.

This is a motorway information sign that tells you that the next exit off
the motorway is 100 metres ahead.

What does this sign mean when displayed on the approach to a motorway?

ABMW3

Cashier in this lane.

This sign is used at motorway toll plazas to direct traffic into a lane
where the toll charge may be paid directly to a cashier. This lane would
normally be used by motorists who have neither the exact change nor
an electronic tag on their vehicle.

What does this sign mean when displayed on the approach to a motorway?

ABMW4

Coin basket in this lane.

This sign is used at motorway toll plazas to direct traffic into a lane
where the toll charge may be paid by putting the exact change into a
coin basket. This lane usually has a height barrier fitted to prevent large
vehicles using it. This lane is generally a quicker way through the toll
plaza than the cashier lane. No change is given at such lanes.

What does this sign mean when displayed on the approach to a motorway?

ABMW5

Electronic toll in this lane.

This sign is used at motorway toll plazas to direct traffic into a lane
where the toll charge is collected electronically. When the vehicle
passes through the plaza it is identified by means of an electronic tag
fitted to the front windscreen. Payment will be collected via the user's
account. Only vehicles fitted with the tags are allowed to use those
lanes.

Road works signs

Road works present a variety of hazards that you need to take into account when you are driving. Always drive with extra care through road works, and take note of the particular signs that are posted.

Like other warning signs, most road works signs are diamond shaped and have a black border and black symbols or text on an orange background.

What does this sign mean?
Roadworks ahead.

ABMW0115

This warning sign tells you that there are roadworks ahead. You should approach with caution and be alert for a change in road surface, and for the presence of machinery and road workers.

What does this sign mean?
Uneven surface ahead.

ABMW0116

This roadworks warning sign tells you that the surface ahead is uneven and you should approach with caution.

What does this sign mean?
Slippery road.

ABMW0117R

This roadworks warning sign tells you that the surface ahead is slippery and that there is an increased risk of skidding.

What does this sign mean?
Road narrows from left.

ABMW0118R

This roadworks warning sign tells you that the road narrows suddenly from the left creating a potential hazard.

What does this sign mean?
Road narrows from right.

ABMW0119R

This roadworks warning sign tells you that the road narrows suddenly from the right creating a potential hazard.

1
2
3

What does this sign mean?
ABMW0120R

Road narrows on both sides.

This roadworks warning sign tells you that the road narrows on both sides creating a potential hazard. Drive with extra care.

What does this sign mean?
ABMW0121R

Flagman ahead.

This roadworks warning sign tells you that the traffic sequence ahead is controlled manually or by an automatic system.

What does this sign mean?
ABMW0122R

Temporary traffic signals ahead.

This roadworks warning sign tells you that temporary traffic signals are in use ahead. You should approach with caution and comply with the signal displayed.

What does this sign mean?
ABMW0123

Two-way traffic.

This roadworks warning sign tells you that there is two-way traffic in operation.

What does this sign mean?
ABMW0124R

Nearside lane of two closed.

This roadworks warning sign tells you that that the lane on the left ahead is closed. If you are in the left lane you will need to move to the right when it is safe to do so.

What does this sign mean?
ABMW0125R

Nearside lane of three closed.

This roadworks warning sign tells you the left-hand lane of three is closed ahead. If you are in the left lane you will need to move to the right when it is safe to do so.

What does this sign mean?
ABMW6
Loose chippings on road.

This roadworks warning sign tells you that the road ahead has been resurfaced and there may be loose chippings. You should reduce speed while driving through this area as the loose chippings could affect your vehicle's road holding and braking.

What does this sign mean?
ABMW0127R
Offside lane closed ahead.

This roadworks warning sign tells you that the extreme right-hand lane is closed ahead. If you are in this lane, you need to move to the left when it is safe to do so. The offside lane is the lane closest to the centre of the road.

What does this sign mean?
ABMW7
Traffic queues likely ahead.

This roadworks warning sign tells you that there may be traffic queues ahead, possibly due to temporary traffic lights at the works. Proceed with caution.

What does this sign mean?
ABMW8
Uneven surface.

This roadworks warning sign tells you that the road surface may be uneven, possibly due to the resurfacing of part of a lane. Proceed with caution.

What does this sign mean?
ABMW0131R
Pedestrians cross to the right.

This roadworks warning sign tells pedestrians to cross to the right as the footpath may be closed at this point.

1
2
3

At roadworks, what does this sign mean?
ABMW0132R

Proceed with caution.

This is the sign telling you to proceed with caution through road works. It may be displayed by a flagman or by an automated system.

At roadworks, what does this sign mean?
ABMW0133R

Stop before or at the sign.

This is a roadworks warning sign telling you to stop. It may be displayed by a flagman or by an automated system.

What do these signs together mean?
ABMW0134

End of detour.

These roadworks warning signs indicate that a detour has ended and that you are back on the original route.

What does this sign mean?
ABMW0135R

Traffic must cross over to the left-hand lane.

This roadworks warning sign tells you that the course of the road will return to the left ahead. This usually appears after a stretch where traffic was diverted to a right-hand lane.

What does this sign mean?
ABMW0136R

Traffic must cross over to the right-hand lane.

This roadworks warning sign tells you that the course of the road will temporarily cross the central reserve to the right.

What does this sign mean?
ABMW0137R

Start of central reserve or obstruction.

This roadworks warning sign tells you that two-way traffic will separate to avoid an obstruction.

What does this sign mean?
ABMW0138R

End of central reserve or obstruction.

This roadworks warning sign tells you that traffic that was separated will revert to two-way road.

Hand signals

You need to be able to interpret correctly the hand signals that other road users make, and there are times when you might need to give clear hand signals.

You also need to know the meaning of hand signals given by a garda.

What does this hand signal mean?
ABMW0140R

The cyclist intends to move out or turn right.

This hand signal tells other road users that the cyclist intends to either move out or make a right turn.

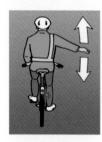

What does this hand signal mean?
ABMW0141R

The cyclist intends to slow down or stop.

This hand signal informs other road users that cyclist intends to slow down or stop. This may indicate that the cyclist is aware of some hazard ahead, so drive with extra care.

What does this hand signal mean?
ABMW0142R

The cyclist intends to go straight on.

This hand signal informs other road users that the cyclist intends to proceed straight ahead at a junction and drivers should show caution.

What does this hand signal mean?
ABMW0143R

The cyclist intends to turn left.

This hand signal informs other road users that the cyclist intends to make a left-hand turn.

1
2
3

What does this hand signal mean?
ABMW0144R

The cyclist intends to turn right.

This hand signal informs other road users that the cyclist intends to turn right.

What does this hand signal mean?
ABMW0145R

The cyclist intends to turn left.

This hand signal informs other road users that the cyclist intends to turn left.

What does this hand signal mean?
ABMW0146R

The driver intends to turn left.

This hand signal informs other road users that the driver intends to turn left and the vehicle will change direction.

What does this hand signal mean?
ABMW0147R

The driver intends to move out or turn right.

This hand signal informs other road users that the driver intends to move out or turn right and the vehicle will change direction.

What does this hand signal mean?
ABMW0148R

The driver intends to slow down or stop.

This hand signal informs other road users that the driver intends to slow down or stop and following traffic should be prepared to slow down also.

What does this hand signal mean? <small>ABMW0149R</small>
The driver intends to turn left.

This hand signal informs other road users or a garda directing traffic (facing this vehicle), that the driver intends to make a left hand turn.

What does this hand signal mean? <small>ABMW0150R</small>
The driver intends to turn right.

This hand signal informs other road users or a garda directing traffic (facing this vehicle) that the driver intends to turn right.

What does this hand signal mean? <small>ABMW0151R</small>
The driver intends to move straight ahead.

This hand signal informs other road users or a garda directing traffic that the driver intends to proceed straight ahead.

1
2
3

What does this Garda signal mean? <small>ABMW0152R</small>
Stop if approaching from the front.

When approaching a garda giving this signal you must stop.

What does this Garda signal mean? <small>ABMW0153R</small>
Stop if approaching from behind.

When approaching a garda giving this signal you must stop.

What does this Garda signal mean?
ABMW0154R

Stop if approaching from either the front or behind.

When approaching a garda giving this signal you must stop.

What does this Garda signal mean?
ABMW0155R

The Garda is beckoning on traffic approaching from either side.

When approaching a garda giving this signal you may proceed.

What does this Garda signal mean?
ABMW0156R

Traffic approaching from the front may proceed.

When approaching a garda giving this signal you may proceed.

1
2
3

Road markings

In addition to knowing what all the regulatory road signs mean, you also have to understand the meaning of road markings and act accordingly.

What does this road marking indicate?
Zebra crossing. ABMW0157R

A zebra crossing is a designated area for pedestrians to cross the road. As a driver you must always yield to pedestrians on a zebra crossing.

What does this road marking mean? ABMW0159R
No parking in this area.

White zig zag lines indicate that you are approaching a pedestrian crossing. You must not park or overtake within this area.

What does this road marking mean?
A driver must not enter unless turning right or the exit is clear.
ABMW0160

You must not enter the yellow box junction unless you can clear it without stopping or unless you are turning right and are prevented from doing so by oncoming traffic.

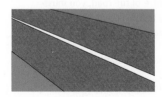

What does this road marking mean? ABMW0161
A driver must not cross the line.

Where there is a continuous white line in the centre of the road, you are not permitted to: 1. Straddle or cross the white line; 2. Overtake another vehicle; 3. Perform a U-turn; or 4. Park on the road this this point.

What does this road marking and information plate together mean?

ABMW0163R

Parking not allowed at the times shown.

**Luan - Aoine
0700 - 0930
MON. - FRI.**

A single yellow line along the edge of a road means that you must not park there during the times shown on the accompanying information plate.

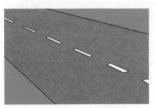

What does this road marking mean?

ABMW0165R

A driver must not cross the broken white line unless it is safe to do so.

A broken white line along the centre of the road means you must not cross the line unless it is safe to do so when overtaking or passing.

What could this road marking mean?

ABMW0166R

Continuous white lines ahead.

Double broken white lines along the centre of the road alert you to continuous white lines ahead. Do not cross them unless it is safe to do so.

B

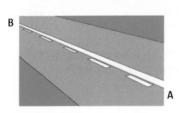

If driving from A to B, what do these road markings mean?

ABMW0167R

A driver may overtake if it is safe to do so.

A

Where there is a broken white line and a continuous white line along the centre of the road, you must obey the line that is nearest to you. In this case you may cross the lines as long as it is safe to do so.

1

2

3

If driving from A to B, what do these road markings mean?
ABMW0168R

A driver may not cross the lines to overtake.

Where there is a broken white line and a continuous white line along the centre of the road, you must obey the line that is nearest to you. In this case you may not cross the lines .

What does this road marking mean?
ABMW0169R

No entry.

This road marking indicates the 'wrong' end of a one-way street. You may not enter this street.

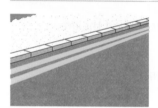

What does this road marking mean?
ABMW0170

Parking prohibited at all times.

A double yellow line along the edge of the road means parking is not allowed at any time.

What does this road marking mean?
ABMW0171R

Drivers must keep left of the continuous white line.

A single continuous white line along the centre of the road means all traffic must keep to the left of the line. You are not permitted to overtake or perform a U-turn on this section of road.

What does the broken yellow line road marking mean?
ABMW0172R

The edge of the carriageway or hard shoulder.

A single broken yellow line along the side of the road marks the edge of the carriageway/hard shoulder. This is normally for the use of pedestrians and cyclists. As a driver, however, you may use it briefly to allow faster traffic to overtake, but only where it is safe to do so.

1
2
3

Traffic lights

You need to know the meaning of all traffic light signals, including those with filter arrows.

What does this traffic light mean?

ABMW0173R

Stop, unless it is unsafe to do so.

When the traffic light is showing amber you must not go beyond the stop line unless you so close to the traffic lights that stopping would be dangerous.

What does this traffic light mean?

ABMW0174R

The driver may proceed in the direction of the green arrow if the way is clear.

A green arrow (filter light) means that traffic may proceed in the direction of the arrow if it is safe to do so.

What does this traffic light mean?

ABMW0175

Left turning traffic may proceed if the way is clear.

A green arrow (filter light) means that traffic may proceed in the direction of the arrow if it is safe to do so.

What does this traffic light mean?

ABMW0176R

Traffic must stop at the traffic light.

A red light means STOP. You must not go beyond the stop line or (if there is no stop line) beyond the light.

What does this traffic light mean?
ABMW0177R

Traffic may proceed if the way is clear.

You may proceed on a green traffic light if it is safe to do so.

What colour traffic light comes on after the green?
ABMW0178R

Amber only.

The normal sequence of traffic lights is red–green–amber.

When traffic lights are green, when should a driver not proceed?
ABMW0179R

When by doing so the vehicle would block the junction.

Although a green traffic light means proceed with caution, you should not enter a junction if the way is not clear or if by doing so you would cause an obstruction to other road users.

What does a flashing left amber arrow at a traffic light mean?
ABMW0180R

A driver may turn left but yield to traffic on the other road.

A flashing left amber arrow at a junction means you may proceed left but must give way to pedestrians and traffic already coming through the junction on the other road.

What colour traffic light comes on after a non-flashing amber light?
Red only.
ABMW0181R

The normal sequence of traffic lights is red–green–amber.

What do flashing amber lights at a pelican crossing mean?
ABMW0182

Stop and give way to pedestrians – proceed if the way is clear.

A flashing amber light at a pelican crossing means you must yield to pedestrians. You may proceed, however, if the crossing is clear.

1
2
3

Speed limits

You must know the speed limits that apply to different types of road and to different types of vehicle. Always drive at a speed that is safe and appropriate to the road you are on. Never exceed the posted speed limits.

What is the maximum permissible speed for cars or motorcycles on motorways?
ABMW0183

120km/h.

It is illegal to exceed 120km/h when driving on a motorway.

What is the maximum permissible speed for cars or motorcycles on single carriageway national roads?
ABMW0184R

100km/h.

It is illegal to exceed 100km/h when driving on a single carriageway national road.

What is the maximum permissible speed of a car towing a caravan on national roads?
ABMW0185R

80km/h.

When towing a caravan on a national road, it is illegal to exceed 80 Km/h – excessive speed will make such a vehicle unstable.

What is the maximum permissible speed of a car towing a caravan on a motorway?
ABMW0186

80km/h.

When towing a caravan on a motorway it is illegal to exceed 80 Km/h – excessive speed will make such a vehicle unstable.

What is the maximum permissible speed of a car towing a trailer on national primary roads?
ABMW0187

80km/h.

When towing a trailer on a national primary road, it is illegal to exceed 80 Km/h – exceeding this speed will make the vehicle unstable,

What is the maximum permissible speed of a car towing a trailer on a motorway?
ABMW0188

80km/h.

When towing a trailer on a motorway it is illegal to exceed 80 Km/h – excessive speed will make such a vehicle unstable.

1
2
3

Regulations relating to parking

Before you park a vehicle, you need to make sure that it is safe and legal to do so in the place you have chosen. A vehicle parked in an inappropriate place may be a serious hazard to other road users. Make sure you know all of the regulations relating to parking.

Where must a driver not park?

ABMW0189R

Where there is a continuous white line along the centre of the road.

It is an offence to park at the side of a road that has a single or double continuous white line along its centre. Parking on such a road could create an obstruction and may cause inconvenience or danger to other road users.

For what distance before a zebra crossing is parking prohibited?

15 metres.

ABMW0190R

It is an offence to park 15 metres before or 5 metres beyond a pedestrian crossing. Parking in this manner may restrict the zone of vision of drivers approaching the crossing and endanger pedestrians.

Within what distance of a junction is parking prohibited?

ABMW0191R

5 metres.

It is an offence to park within 5 metres of a road junction unless parking spaces are clearly marked. Parking in that area may restrict the zone of vision of drivers approaching the junction and may cause an obstruction to large vehicles wishing to turn.

When may a driver park a vehicle in a loading bay?

ABMW0192R

When the driver is the driver of a goods vehicle and is loading or unloading.

Loading bays are provided to enable goods vehicles to load or unload goods, up to a maximum of 30 minutes. Only goods vehicles are permitted to use loading bays.

Is a driver permitted to park at an entrance to a property?

ABMW0193R

Yes, with the property owner's consent.

You may park across the entrance to a property only with the owner's consent. Parking across an entrance may cause inconvenience and danger to persons entering or leaving the property.

When is parking permitted on a footpath?

ABMW0194R

It is never permitted to park on a footpath.

It is always an offence to park on a footpath. Where a vehicle is parked on a footpath, pedestrians may have to step onto the road to go around the vehicle and so place themselves in danger.

When is double parking permitted?

ABMW0195R

Double parking is never permitted.

Double parking is never permitted. Parking is never permitted where it might interfere in any way with the normal flow of traffic or obstruct or endanger other road users.

When is parking permitted at a taxi rank?

ABMW0196R

Parking at a taxi rank is prohibited.

Stopping or parking within an area marked as a taxi rank is prohibited as this may obstruct taxis entering or leaving the rank.

When is parking permitted at a sharp bend?

ABMW0197R

Parking is never permitted at a sharp bend.

Parking is never permitted where it might interfere in any way with the normal flow of traffic or obstruct or endanger other road users for example, by forcing other drivers into the path of oncoming traffic.

When is parking permitted on the brow of a hill?

ABMW0198R

Parking on the brow of a hill is never allowed.

Parking on the brow of a hill or on a humpbacked bridge is prohibited. Parking in such a place may restrict the zone of vision of drivers approaching the hill and force them into the path of oncoming traffic.

1

2

3

Regulations relating to pedestrians

Pedestrians are the most vulnerable road users, and as a driver you need to be extra careful where there are pedestrians.

If there is no footpath, where must a pedestrian walk?
ABMW0199R
Right-hand side of the road.

Where there is no footpath provided, pedestrians should walk on the right-hand side of the road facing oncoming traffic. Drivers should be aware of the *Rules of the Road* for pedestrians, drive with caution and be prepared to react to any changes in the traffic situation.

On a narrow busy road, what rules apply to pedestrians when walking?
Walk in single file.
ABMW0203R

Pedestrians should walk in single file on busy narrow roads. Drivers should be aware of the *Rules of the Road* for pedestrians, drive with caution and be prepared to react to any changes in the traffic situation.

When should pedestrians wear reflective clothing at night?
ABMW0204R
At all times outside well-lit urban areas.

Outside built-up areas, pedestrians should wear reflective clothing at all times when walking at night. This is particularly important where there is no street lighting and no footpath for pedestrians.

What road users must comply with traffic lights (including pedestrian lights)?
ABMW0205R
All road users.

As road users, pedestrians must comply with traffic controls. Drivers should be aware that traffic lights and pedestrian lights can be combined at junctions and should show caution and consideration to pedestrians.

1
2
3

Other regulatory matters

There are a number of other regulatory matters that you need to know about. Mostly these are regulations that guide our behaviour and help ensure the safety of all road users.

When are lighting up hours?
ABMW0207R

From just after dusk to just before dawn.

Lighting up hours are defined as the period of time during which drivers should turn on dipped headlights in order to be seen. This period normally starts half an hour after sunset and ends half an hour before sunrise.

What lights should a vehicle show at dusk?
ABMW0208R

Dipped headlights.

Drivers need to see and be seen during all periods of low light levels – for example, at dusk and dawn and in some bad weather conditions. At times of low light, you should turn on dipped headlights.

The Road Safety Authority recommends that motorcyclists and drivers turn on their dipped headlights or daytime running lights during daylight hours.

What do rumble strips warn a driver of?
ABMW0209R

A danger immediately ahead or to the side.

Rumble strips are a patterning in the surface of the roadway that causes a rumbling sound when you drive over them. The purpose of them is to warn you to of a potential danger ahead or to the side.

What is the purpose of traffic calming measures?
ABMW0210R

To slow down traffic in the vicinity.

The purpose of traffic calming measures is to slow down fast-moving traffic to a speed more suitable for the area they are entering. These measures are usually found in rural areas on the entry points to towns or villages.

1

2

3

When may a trailer be towed on a public road without a rear number plate?
ABMW0211R

Never, a number plate must always be displayed.

The law requires all motorised vehicles to display a rear number plate that is clean and legible.

When may a driver pass another vehicle on the left-hand side?
ABMW0212R

When the vehicle in front is signalling to turn right or in slow moving lanes of traffic.

Normally you must overtake on the right. There are, however, circumstances where you may overtake on the left – for example, when the vehicle has moved out and signalled to turn right.

Who can use a signed cycle track accompanied by a continuous white line on the left-hand side?
ABMW0213R

Cyclists and users of motorised wheelchairs.

A cycle track is for the use of cyclists and motorised wheelchairs only. No other vehicles may cross into or over a mandatory cycle track unless this is necessary in order to leave or enter a side road or a property adjacent to the cycle track.

What traffic may drive along on a cycle lane accompanied by a continuous white line?
ABMW0214R

Cyclists and motorised wheelchairs.

A cycle track is for the use of cyclists and motorised wheelchairs. No other vehicles may cross into or over a mandatory cycle track unless this is necessary in order to leave a side road or a property adjacent to the cycle track.

What traffic may drive along on a cycle lane accompanied by a broken white line?
ABMW0215R

Cyclists and users of motorised wheelchairs.

A cycle track is for the use of cyclists and motorised wheelchairs only. No other vehicles may cross into or over a mandatory cycle track unless this is necessary in order to leave or enter a side road or a property adjacent to the cycle track.

1
2
3

When must drivers stop at a railway level crossing controlled by lights and barriers?
ABMW0216R

When the red lights start to flash.

You are legally required to stop at a level crossing when the red lights start to flash and the warning bells sound. You must wait for all barriers to open fully before proceeding.

At a level crossing with unattended gates, what should a driver do?
Open both gates before proceeding to cross.
ABMW0217R

At a level crossing with unattended gates a driver must stop, look for trains and listen for the sound of a horn or approaching trains. If it is safe, open both gates, complete the crossing and then close both gates.

What lights indicate a zebra crossing?
ABMW0218R

Flashing amber beacons.

A zebra crossing is indicated by amber flashing beacons on poles and black and white stripes on the road. You must stop for pedestrians on the crossing and for those about to cross.

What do flashing amber arrows indicate?
ABMW0219R

Drivers should proceed in the direction indicated.

When you meet a flashing amber arrow, you should proceed in the direction indicated provided it is safe to do so. Large flashing amber arrows can be found at roadworks on dual carriageways and motorways.

What do temporary traffic lights at road works mean?
ABMW0220R

A driver must comply with the lights at all times.

You must comply with any temporary traffic lights used to control vehicle movements at or near road works. It is an offence not to obey these lights.

When do temporary speed limits apply at roadworks?
ABMW0221R

For the duration of the roadworks.

Temporary speed limits at road works apply for a limited period of time. When road works are completed, normal speed limits apply.

Alert driving and consideration for other road users

When you are driving, the traffic situation is changing constantly, and different kinds of hazard can arise with or without warning. You need to remain alert at all times and show consideration for all other road users.

The questions in this section test your knowledge in a number of areas:

1

2

3

Illustrated traffic situations	These are typical of the kind of situations that you need to be alert to when driving.
Anticipation of hazards	Anticipation skills help you identify and avoid hazards on the road.
Consideration for other road users	Good drivers always display consideration for other road users.
Alertness to danger	You need to remain alert to potential danger at all times.

Illustrated traffic situations

Every time you go on the road you meet different traffic situations and potential hazards, and you need to maintain your concentration at all times so that you will make the right and safe decisions every time.

What is the correct action to take in this situation?
ABMW0222R

Keep a close eye on children. If necessary give a warning signal and be prepared to brake in good time.

Because it is difficult to predict children's behaviour, you should always be prepared to react to a change in the traffic situation or to stop.

1

2

3

An approaching driver notices that the boy on the children's bicycle has said goodbye to his friend. What is the correct action for the driver to take?
ABMW0223R

Be prepared for the boy setting off at any moment without paying attention to your vehicle.

Because it is difficult to predict children's behaviour, you should always be prepared to react to a change in the traffic situation or to stop.

As the driver of the car, which conduct is correct?
ABMW0224R

A driver may proceed with caution.

You may proceed, but you should be aware of the presence of the motorcyclist. You should always be prepared to react to a change in the traffic situation – for example, the motorcyclist might not have seen your vehicle.

What should the car driver do in this situation?
ABMW0225R

The driver must allow the cyclist to proceed.

When you are turning right from a major road to a minor road, you must yield to oncoming traffic, and you should proceed only when it is safe to do so.

What must a driver be prepared for in this situation?
ABMW0226R

One of the children could turn back to collect the ball from the roadway.

Because it is difficult to predict children's behaviour, you should always be prepared to react to a change in the traffic situation and be prepared to stop.

When approaching the pedestrian crossing, what should the driver do in this situation?
ABMW0227R

Slow down in good time and be prepared to stop.

When there are pedestrians at or near a zebra crossing, you should slow down on approach and be prepared to stop to allow the pedestrians to cross safely.

What should the driver do in this situation?
ABMW0228R

The driver must yield to the yellow car on the roundabout.

When you reach the roundabout, you must give way to traffic approaching from the right unless signs, road markings or traffic lights tell you otherwise.

1
2
3

What should the car driver do in this situation?
ABMW0229R

The car driver must allow the motorcycle to proceed.

When you are turning right from a major road to a minor road, you must yield to oncoming traffic. You should proceed only when it is safe to do so.

What should the driver do in this situation?
ABMW0230R

The driver may turn in front of the other two cars.

When you are turning right from a major road to a minor road, you must yield to oncoming traffic and only proceed when it is safe to do so. However, the drivers on the minor roads must give way to the traffic on the major road.

What should a driver be alert to in this area?
ABMW0231R

Pedestrians may cross between parked cars.

When driving in a built-up area, you should drive with caution and be prepared to react to pedestrians crossing from between parked vehicles.

What should the driver do if there are children playing at the edge of the roadway?
ABMW0232R

Reduce speed, drive cautiously and remain ready to brake.

Because it is difficult to predict children's behaviour, you should always be prepared to react to a change in the traffic situation and be prepared to stop.

What should the driver do in this situation?

ABMW0233R

The driver may cross first with caution.

On approaching a crossroads you should check the road sign to see which traffic has priority and be prepared for emerging traffic from either side. Vehicles do not have an automatic right of way on the road. The overriding rule is to proceed with caution in all circumstances.

What should the driver do in this situation?

ABMW0234R

The driver may proceed first.

You may turn right if there no oncoming traffic but you should also be aware that there might be traffic emerging from the minor roads.

What should the driver do in this situation?

ABMW0235R

The driver must allow the blue truck to proceed.

When you are turning right from a major road to a minor road, you must yield to oncoming traffic and proceed only when it is safe to do so. You should also be aware that there might be emerging from the minor road.

What should a driver be conscious of in this situation?

ABMW0236R

People crossing the street at the rear of the bus.

You should always read the road ahead and be prepared to react to the changing traffic situation. In particular, you should be aware that pedestrians might emerge at the rear of the bus. In this situation you should also look out for pedestrians making their way towards the waiting Bus

1
2
3

The silver car is overtaking the parked red car, what should the driver do in this situation?
ABMW0237R

Reduce speed considerably and be ready to stop.

You should read the road and be extra careful while driving through an area where children might be playing. When a ball bounces out on the road you should expect that a child might follow to retrieve the ball.

What should a driver be aware of in this situation?
ABMW0238R

Pedestrians may leave the traffic island without paying attention.

You should read the road ahead and expect extra pedestrian activity when the tram is at the stop.

The driver is following these two vehicles and wishes to overtake - what must the driver consider before overtaking here?
ABMW0239R

The driver's field of view is not good enough to allow safe overtaking.

You should always make sure that the road ahead is clear so that there is enough distance to allow you to overtake and get back to the correct side of the road without forcing any other road user to alter speed or course. In this case, the brow of the hill is too close to allow a driver to overtake safely.

What should a driver be aware of when approaching a vehicle which is attempting to park?
ABMW0240R

That the vehicle being parked may move out without warning.

When you approach a vehicle that is being parked on the roadway, you should be aware that its driver will probably be concentrating on parking the vehicle and may not be aware of moving out into the road to correct its position.

1

2

3

What should the driver allow for when following the bus on an icy road?
A longer braking distance.

ABMW0241R

When driving in icy conditions, you should always reduce speed and allow a bigger gap to the vehicle in front in order to be able to stop safely if necessary.

ABMW0242R

What should the driver of the silver car do before turning left?
Allow the cyclist heading straight on to pass.

Do not overtake a cyclist as you approach a junction at which you are turning left. The cyclist might be continuing ahead. Cyclists are vulnerable road users and may be unstable in slow-moving traffic and at junctions. Give them more room.

What lights should a driver use in fog?
Front and rear fog lights along with dipped headlights.

ABMW0246R

When driving in fog you should switch on your front and rear fog lights along with dipped headlights. You should not drive in fog with full beam headlights on.

What should the driver be most conscious of in this situation?

ABMW0248R

The pedestrian may suddenly cross the road in front of the vehicle.

It is often difficult to predict other road users' behaviour. Where there are parked vehicles on both sides of the road you should approach with caution, and be prepared to react to a change in the traffic situation and to stop.

What should the driver do when approaching this situation?

ABMW0249R

Reduce speed and remain ready to brake since the girl on foot could suddenly cross the road.

It is often difficult to predict other road users' behaviour. You should be prepared in case the pedestrian steps onto the road and the silver car stops suddenly.

What should the driver do?

ABMW0250R

The driver should allow the yellow car to proceed.

At a cross junction of equal importance the traffic approaching from the right has priority. It is important to understand that the right of way is not an absolute right. You must proceed with caution while showing regard for other road users.

Which car, if any, is parked incorrectly?

Both cars.

ABMW0251

It is an offence to park within 15 metres before or 5 metres after a pedestrian crossing. Parking in this manner may restrict the zone of vision of drivers approaching the crossing and endanger pedestrians.

What should a driver be aware of in this situation?

ABMW0252R

The cyclist will move onto the roadway without paying attention to moving traffic.

You should show extra care when approaching cyclists who are about to exit from a cycle lane and join the roadway.

A driver wants to pull out of a driveway and turn right onto the road. At the same time a cyclist is approaching from the right and a pedestrian wants to cross. Who must wait?

The driver must wait.   ABMW0253R

By law you must give way to other road users, including pedestrians and cyclists, when you are entering or leaving a driveway.

What action should the driver take?

Stop at the Stop line.   ABMW0254R

By law you must stop at a Stop line (or at a Stop sign if there is no Stop line), and wait for other traffic to clear before proceeding.

What should a driver do when travelling behind this vehicle?   ABMW0255R

Reduce speed and prepare to stop if necessary.

You should always read the road ahead and be prepared to react to the changing traffic situation as you approach junctions.

What does a continuous white line along the centre of the road mean?   ABMW0256R

No u-turn allowed.

You must never do a U-turn on any stretch of road with a continuous white line along its centre. The restricted vision at such places would make doing a U-turn very unsafe.

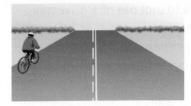

How should a driver overtake the cyclist in this situation?
ABMW0257R

By crossing the broken white line.

Where there are two lines in the centre of the road, you must obey the one closest to you. So, if the closest line is a broken white line, by law you may overtake, so long as it is safe to do so.

What does a white line in the centre of the road mean?
ABMW0259R

Vehicles may not cross or straddle the line.

1

2

3

You must not cross or straddle a continuous white line in the centre of the road unless you wish to enter land or premises and it is safe to do so.

The driver intends to turn left at this junction – what should the driver do?
Allow the cyclist to continue before turning left.
ABMW0261R

Do not overtake a cyclist as you approach a junction at which you are turning left. The cyclist might be continuing ahead. Cyclists are vulnerable road users and may be unstable in slow-moving traffic and at junctions. Give them more room.

Why might it be dangerous to drive on a poorly-lit street?
ABMW0262R

Pedestrians crossing in a dark area might be difficult to see.

When you are driving along a poorly-lit street, you should take extra care – vulnerable road users such as pedestrians might not be so easy to see. You should always be prepared to react to a change in the traffic situation.

Why might it be dangerous to drive on a poorly-lit street?
ABMW0263R

It may be difficult to make out poorly lit vehicles in the dark areas.

When you are driving along a poorly-lit street, you should take extra care and be prepared to react to hazards such as unlit parked vehicles.

The driver intends to turn right at this junction - what should the driver do?

Proceed after the bus and motorcycle have passed.
ABMW0264R

When you are turning right at a junction, you should yield to traffic on the major road, and to oncoming traffic at the junction.

The driver intends to turn right at this junction - what should the driver do?

Stop at the line.
ABMW0265R

You must stop at the line where a junction is controlled by a Stop sign and Stop line. Do not proceed until it is safe to do so.

What should a driver do if dazzled by the lights of an oncoming vehicle?
ABMW0266R

Look to the left-hand edge of the roadway and if necessary reduce speed.

If you are dazzled by the lights of oncoming traffic, turn your eyes to the left edge of the road. If necessary, stop and allow your eyes to recover before driving on.

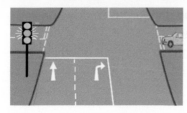

What should a driver do when approaching traffic lights that change from green to amber?
Stop, unless it is unsafe to do so. ABMW0268R

When you are approaching a set of traffic lights showing green, you should take care and be prepared to stop if the amber light comes on.

When intending to turn right as shown, what should the car driver do?
Wait and allow the oncoming vehicle to pass. ABMW0270R

When you are turning right from a main road onto a side road, you must by law give way to oncoming traffic on the main road.

When intending to turn right as shown, what should the car driver do?
Proceed before the truck. ABMW0271R

When you are driving on a main road, you have priority over traffic emerging from side roads. But it is important to understand that the right of way is not an absolute right and you must proceed with caution and showing regard for other road users.

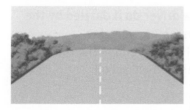

What danger should a driver allow for over the brow of this hill? ABMW0272R
There may be a slow moving vehicle in your lane.

On the approach to the brow of a hill you should be extra careful and be prepared to react to a change in the traffic situation.

1
2
3

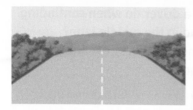

What danger should a driver allow for over the brow of this hill?

ABMW0273R

A vehicle may be broken down.

On the approach to the brow of a hill you should be extra careful and be prepared to react to a change in the traffic situation.

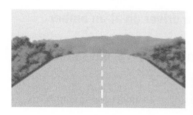

What danger should a driver allow for over the brow of this hill?

ABMW0275R

There may be oncoming pedestrians.

On the approach to the brow of a hill you should be extra careful and be prepared to react to a change in the traffic situation.

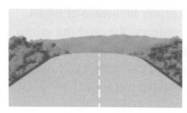

What danger should a driver allow for over the brow of this hill?

ABMW0276R

There may be livestock on the road.

On approach to the brow of a hill you should be extra careful and be prepared to react to a change in the traffic situation.

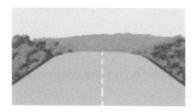

What danger should a driver allow for over the brow of this hill?

ABMW0277R

There may be hedge-cutting taking place.

On the approach to the brow of a hill you should be extra careful and be prepared to react to a change in the traffic situation.

What should a driver be aware of in this situation?

ABMW0278R

There may be a car hidden from view in front of the bus.

On approach to an area with a restricted view you should be extra careful and be prepared to react to a change in the traffic situation.

1
2
3

What should a driver do when continuing straight ahead in the middle lane? ABMW0279R
Slow down and allow the driver in front to change lanes.

You should always keep a safe distance from the vehicle in front especially when it is slowing down or stopping.

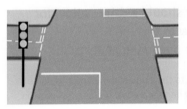

What should a driver do at an amber traffic light. ABMW0280R
Stop at the line unless it is not safe to do so.

By law you must stop at an amber traffic light if it is safe to do so.

1
2
3

What should a driver be aware of when following the motorcyclist, and the white car is reversing onto the road? ABMW0282R
The driver following the motorcycle may need a longer braking distance than normal.

You should always keep a safe distance from the vehicle in front if it is slowing down or stopping. Always read the road and be prepared to react correctly to changes in the traffic ahead.

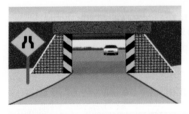

What should a driver do on the approach to this situation? ABMW0283R
Reduce speed and stop if necessary.

When road priority is unclear you might have to yield to oncoming vehicles. Never drive a vehicle into an area that it might not be able to clear or where it could cause an obstruction or bottleneck.

When driving on a cobblestone road why should you take extra care? ABMW0285R

The road surface is uneven and road grip varies.

Different road surfaces can affect your vehicle's grip on the road and its stopping distances. You should be aware of this when driving on different surfaces.

When driving on a road with tram lines why should a driver take extra care? ABMW12

Driving on the tracks can reduce tyre grip.

Different road surfaces can affect your vehicle's grip on the road and its stopping distances. You should be aware of this when driving on different surfaces.

1
2
3

After a heavy downpour, why should a driver keep a greater distance from the vehicle in front? ABMW0286R

Because wheel-spray may impair visibility.

Heavy rain can affect how well you can see and how well you can be seen by other road users. Because of that you should slow down in heavy rain and keep a greater distance from the vehicle in front.

When driving on this one-way street with vehicles parked on both sides, what should a driver be prepared for? ABMW0287R

A vehicle door may open on either side of the street.

When driving on a one-way street, you should be extra careful and should be prepared to react to a change in the traffic situation.

When driving on this one-way street with vehicles parked on both sides, what should a driver be prepared for? ABMW0288R
Pedestrians crossing between the vehicles.

When driving on a one-way street, you should be extra careful and be prepared to react to a change in the traffic situation.

Why must a driver be particularly careful here? ABMW0289R
Because there is an increased danger of skidding.

Where there are fallen leaves on the road surface, your tyres might have reduced grip on the road surface and your braking distances might be greater.

What should a driver do in this situation when intending to turn left? ABMW0290R
Wait and allow both pedestrians to cross.

By law you must yield to pedestrians already crossing at a junction. Pedestrians are vulnerable road users and you should be extra careful driving at places where pedestrians are attempting to cross the road.

What should a driver do when turning right at this junction? ABMW0291R
Allow the red car to proceed.

When you are turning right from a main road into a side road, you must give way to oncoming traffic on the main road even if they are turning left into the same road.

What should the car driver be aware of in this situation?
ABMW0292R

Oncoming traffic may cut the corner.

When you are approaching a bend or corner with a restricted view you should slow down if necessary and be prepared to react to any changes in the traffic situation.

What should the car driver be aware of in this situation?
ABMW0293R

Animals could suddenly appear on the road ahead.

When you are approaching a bend or corner with a restricted view you should slow down if necessary and be prepared to react to any changes in the traffic situation.

What should a driver be aware of when driving at night along a shopping street with many different light sources?
ABMW0294R

Traffic lights may be difficult to distinguish from the other bright lights.

When driving at night in an area where there is a variety of light sources, you need to be extra careful, as potential hazards might be more difficult to see.

What should a driver be most aware of in this situation?
ABMW0295R

Children may unexpectedly run out from between parked cars.

When driving in a residential area you need to take account of the danger you might pose to children playing. You should always observe warning signs relating to children and drive accordingly.

1
2
3

What should a driver do in this situation?
Reduce speed and be prepared to stop as other children could follow. ABMW0296R

You should always be aware of other road users especially children, who can be unpredictable and show no road sense. You should drive with extra care in areas where there are children about for example, near schools, playgrounds and in residential areas.

In this situation who should wait?
The driver behind the stopped van should wait. ABMW0297R

When you are overtaking a parked vehicle or obstruction, you should yield to oncoming vehicles so that they don't have to slow down or take evasive action.

In this situation, who should wait?
The driver in the red car should wait. ABMW0298R

A vehicle driving on the main road has priority over vehicles emerging from side roads. However, you must understand that the right of way is not an absolute right of way and you should be considerate of other road users at all times.

What should a driver do in this situation?
Allow the pedestrian to cross the road.

ABMW0302R

When approaching a zebra crossing, you must yield to pedestrians already on or about to cross the road.

What should a driver be aware of in this situation?
A dangerous right-hand bend ahead.

ABMW0304R

You should always read the road ahead and be prepared to react to changing traffic situations – in this case paying attention to the warning sign clearly indicating a right-hand bend ahead.

What should a driver who wants to turn right do in this situation?
ABMW0306R

Proceed straight ahead or turn left.

As you approach a junction where you want to turn right, you should read the road ahead and take up the correct position for turning in good time.

1
2
3

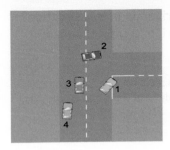

Which vehicle is in the correct position to make a right turn from the major road into the minor road?

ABMW0307R

3

The correct position from which to turn right from a major road to a minor road is just left of centre. You should take up the correct position in good time and avoid cutting the corner or 'swan necking' – that is going beyond the turning point as car 2 is in the picture.

Which vehicle is in the correct position to make a right turn from a minor road onto a major road?

ABMW0312R

1

The correct position from which to turn right from a minor road to a major road is just left of centre of the road. You should take up the correct position in good time and complete the turn by entering the left-hand side of the major road.

Driver behaviour and anticipation

Having good anticipation skills means scanning the road ahead and always being aware of the potential for hazards.

After a heavy downpour, why should a driver keep a greater distance from the vehicle in front?

ABMW13

Because stopping distances are greater.

On a wet road surface, your tyres do not grip the road surface as well as in dry conditions and your stopping distance is increased. Because of that you should slow down during or after rain and keep a greater distance from the vehicle in front.

What should the driver do when there is a sharp dip in the road ahead?

Reduce speed, keep to the left and be alert for hazards ahead. ABMW0314R

As you approach a sharp dip in the road, you should be aware that there might be hidden dangers ahead. For example, there might be pedestrians, cyclists or other approaching traffic, or the road could be flooded in the dip. You should always read the road ahead and be prepared to react to changing traffic situations – you might need to reduce your speed and drive with extra care.

What should a driver do if they see a red warning triangle on the road?

The driver should slow down and expect a hazard up ahead. ABMW0315R

Warning triangles are used to alert approaching traffic that there is a vehicle breakdown or collision ahead. When you come across a warning triangle, you should slow down and be prepared to stop if necessary. Do not allow yourself to be distracted by the incident.

The driver is approaching traffic lights that they know have been green for some time. What should the driver do? ABMW0316R

The driver should prepare to stop in case the lights change before they reach them.

You should always read the road ahead and be prepared to react to changing traffic situations. Where traffic lights have been green for some time, you should be prepared to stop, as the lights are probably about to change to amber.

What should a driver do when approaching a junction normally controlled by traffic lights and the traffic lights are not lighting? ABMW0317R

Treat the junction as an unmarked junction and proceed cautiously while watching out for other traffic.

You should always read the road ahead and be prepared to react to changing traffic situations. If the traffic lights are not working, you should approach the junction with extra care, and you should proceed only if it is safe to do so.

1
2
3

What should the driver do if there are cattle on the road ahead?

The driver should reduce speed and overtake with care. ABMW0318R

You should always read the road ahead and be prepared to react to changing traffic situations. If you meet cattle or other animals on the road, you should slow down and be prepared to stop . Don't use the horn or do anything that might frighten the animals. You must stop if directed to do so by the person in charge of animals.

What should a driver do if they see horse riders on the road ahead?

The driver should reduce speed and allow extra clearance and pass with care. ABMW0319R

You should always read the road ahead and be prepared to react to changing traffic situations. If you meet horses or other animals on the road, you should slow down and be prepared to stop . Don't use the horn or do anything that might frighten the animals. You must stop if directed to do so by the person in charge of animals.

What should drivers be aware of if they meet horses with riders on the road? ABMW0320R

Drivers should be aware that loud noises from their vehicle may frighten the horses and cause them to bolt.

You must know your responsibilities towards animal traffic on the road. Horses are easily startled and any sudden noises or activity could cause them to bolt.

What should the driver do when approaching a humpbacked hill?

The driver should reduce speed, keep to the left and be alert for hazards ahead. ABMW0321R

As you approach a humpbacked bridge or hill, you should be aware that there might be hidden dangers ahead – for example, overtaking traffic coming towards you. You should always read the road ahead and be prepared to react to changing traffic situations such as this.

What should a driver do if there is a large oil spill on the road?

Reduce speed by gently applying the brakes and switch on the hazard warning lights. ABMW0322R

Where oil is spilt on the road, your tyres will have reduced grip, and you might be at risk of skidding if you brake sharply. If you do come across oil on the road, brake gently and switch on your hazard warning lights for a short period to alert other traffic to the hazard.

What do flashing amber beacons on an oncoming vehicle alert a driver to?

ABMW0323R

That the oncoming vehicle may be slow moving or extra wide.

Flashing amber beacons are used by recovery vehicles and vehicles carrying abnormal loads. You should be aware that these vehicles may need extra room and could conceal following traffic. When you come across such vehicles, slow down and be prepared to stop if necessary.

What should a driver do if they meet a vehicle with flashing amber beacons?

ABMW0324R

Slow down and prepare to stop.

Flashing amber beacons are used by recovery vehicles and vehicles carrying abnormal loads. You should be aware that these vehicles may need extra room and could conceal following traffic. When you come across such vehicles, slow down and be prepared to stop if necessary.

What should a driver be aware of before crossing railway or tram lines?

There may be an uneven surface and tyre grip may be reduced when crossing the rails.

ABMW0325R

You should be aware of the impact of changes in the road surface. For example, at railway and tram crossings the uneven surface or oil deposits could reduce the grip of your tyres. Slow down as you approach railway or tram crossings and increase your distance from the vehicle in front.

What should the driver be aware of when crossing road markings such as lines and directional arrows?

ABMW0326R

The stopping distance is increased due to reduced tyre grip.

You should be aware of the impact of changes in the road surface. For example, road markings and directional arrows can become slippery when wet. Where possible, avoid driving on road markings, and be aware of the increased risk of skidding.

1
2
3

Consideration for other road users

While driving, you need to show consideration for other road users at all times.

There are pedestrians on the footpath ahead and there are pools of water on the road. What should a driver do?
ABMW0327R

Reduce speed and try to avoid the pools of water so as not to splash the pedestrians.

During wet conditions, you should be aware that surface water can affect the stability of your vehicle. This is particularly so where the water lies in pools. As you drive through surface water, you should show consideration to pedestrians and cyclists and try not to splash them as you pass.

When preparing to stop, a driver notices the vehicle behind is towing a trailer. What should the driver do?
ABMW0328R

Indicate in good time and pull in gradually to allow the vehicle behind extra stopping distance.

When you are slowing down or stopping, you should be mindful of the type of vehicle that is following you. For example, if the vehicle following you is a large vehicle or one towing a trailer, you should think of indicating a little earlier than normal to allow the following vehicle enough time to react safely.

The bus ahead is moving away from a bus stop. What should a driver do?
Slow down and allow it to move out.
ABMW0329R

A driver should allow signalling buses back into the stream of traffic when they are moving out from a stop. Be careful of pedestrians getting on and off buses, particularly of children near schools.

What should a driver do on a narrow road when another vehicle is coming in the opposite direction?
ABMW0330R

Reduce speed and allow reasonable clearance between their vehicle and the oncoming one before proceeding.

You should always be prepared to react to hazards ahead. When you meet a vehicle coming against you on a narrow road, you should show consideration and slow down to a appropriate speed so that the two vehicles can pass each other safely.

1

2

3

When driving along and wishing to stop at a shop on the side of the street in order to make a purchase, what should a driver do?

Continue on to a safe parking space.   ABMW0331R

You may park only where it is safe and legal to do so. Your parked vehicle must not cause a danger or an obstruction to other road users

---

When a driver is driving behind another vehicle that they do not intend to overtake, what should the driver do?   ABMW0332R

Keep well back to allow following traffic to overtake them.

You should always allow sufficient distance between your vehicle and the vehicle in front. This will enable you to stop safely if necessary, and it will give overtaking vehicles enough room to pull in safely to the left lane after they have passed you.

When a driver is driving in a line of traffic and does not intend to overtake, what should the driver do?   ABMW0333R

Stay back and leave a gap for other drivers to overtake.

You should always allow sufficient distance between your vehicle and the vehicle in front. This will enable you to stop safely if necessary, and it will give overtaking vehicles enough room to pull in safely to the left lane after they have passed you.

Why is tailgating (driving too close behind the vehicle in front) dangerous?   ABMW0337R

The vehicle will not have sufficient distance to stop safely in an emergency.

If you drive too close to the vehicle in front and it brakes suddenly, you will not have enough time to react. For that reason you should always keep a safe distance from the vehicle in front. One way of calculating a safe distance is the 'two-second rule': allow at least two seconds to elapse between the vehicle in front and your own vehicle passing a fixed point such as a lamp post or sign post.

Is tailgating allowed on a motorway or dual carriageway?   ABMW0338R

No, because the vehicle in front may stop suddenly.

If you drive too close to the vehicle in front and it brakes suddenly, you will not have enough time to react. For that reason you should always keep a safe distance from the vehicle in front. One way of calculating a safe distance is the 'two-second rule': allow at least two seconds to elapse between the vehicle in front and your own vehicle passing a fixed point such as a lamp post or sign post.

Alertness to danger

Dangerous situations can arise without warning, so you need to be alert at all times to changing road and traffic situations.

What danger can arise during daylight when a driver enters an area that is heavily shaded by overhanging trees? ABMW0339R

Visibility could be suddenly reduced.

When you enter a heavily shaded area after driving in bright sunlight, it might take a while for your eyes to adjust to the change, and you might not see a hazard immediately ahead.

What should a driver do when being overtaken by another vehicle?

Continue at the same pace. ABMW0340R

When you are being overtaken by another vehicle, you should continue at the same pace but be alert in case the overtaking vehicle suddenly pulls back in front you.

When should signals (for example, with indicators) be given to other road users? ABMW0341R

Clearly and in good time to let other road users know your intentions.

Giving signals is a way of telling other road users what you intend to do. So, you should signal properly before moving off, turning right or left, changing lanes, overtaking, slowing down or stopping. Signal clearly and in good time, and keep in mind that giving a signal does not give you the right of way.

When driving into a narrow gap between oncoming vehicles and vehicles parked on the left. What should a driver do? ABMW0342R

Indicate right, stopping if necessary until oncoming traffic has passed by.

When you meet approaching traffic at a narrow gap, you should show consideration and slow down to a appropriate speed so that you and the other vehicles can pass each other safely. If necessary, give way to the other vehicles.

How does giving a late signal affect other road users? ABMW0343R

They may not have sufficient time to react.

Giving signals is a way of telling other road users what you intend to do. So, you should signal properly before moving off, turning right or left, changing lanes, overtaking, slowing down or stopping. Signal clearly and in good time, and keep in mind that giving a signal does not give you the right of way. Late signals may confuse other road users.

1

2

3

Observation and field of view

When you are driving, you must always have a clear picture of the road ahead and the traffic conditions all around you. You should also make sure that other road users can see you, so that they are not taken by surprise and forced to take emergency evasive action.

1

2

3

Visibility

The questions in this section deal with situations where your ability to see the road ahead is restricted and with the effects of rain on your ability to control your vehicle.

How does rain affect driving in this situation?
ABMW0344R
It increases the danger of skidding.

When it is wet, your tyres do not grip the road surface as well as when it is dry, your stopping distance is increased and you are more likely to skid. For these reasons you should slow down during or after rain and keep a greater distance from the vehicle in front.

When a driver is at a junction where visibility is extremely limited, what should the driver do?
ABMW0345R
Move out with extreme care, watching carefully to the left and right.

Where your view is obstructed at a junction, you should move carefully into a position where you can see, but without interfering with other road users. You should then assess the situation before you continue.

When should a driver use the vehicle's rear view mirror?
ABMW0346R
Before changing direction.

You should use your mirrors to stay aware of traffic situations behind and around you. Always check your mirror before you change direction on a road, and before you signal or begin a manoeuvre.

How should a driver proceed if their view is obstructed at a junction?
ABMW0347R
Move out slowly onto the road while watching carefully for other traffic.

At junctions where the view is obstructed, move carefully into a position where you can see without interfering with other road users. Then assess the situation before you continue.

What should a driver do when approaching traffic lights stuck on red?
ABMW0348R

Stop and proceed with great caution.

When you approach a junction with the traffic lights stuck on red, stop at the line, take the required observation and proceed with caution when it is safe to do so. Treat the junction as 'unmarked' and do not assume that you have the right of way.

What should a driver do when there are dark clouds and visibility is reduced during daylight hours?
ABMW0349R

Drive with side-lights or dipped headlights switched on.

Drivers need to see and be seen during all periods of low light levels – for example, at dusk and dawn and in some bad weather conditions. At times of low light, you should turn on dipped headlights.

The Road Safety Authority recommends that motorcyclists and drivers turn on their dipped headlights or daytime running lights during daylight hours.

1

2

3

Blindspots

When driving, you need to be aware of the fact that there are some parts of the road around you that you cannot see easily, either directly or with your mirrors. You need to be sure that these areas are clear of other road users before moving into them. Equally, when travelling behind a truck or other large vehicle, or when overtaking another vehicle, you should be aware that there are times when you are 'invisible' to the other driver.

When driving behind a heavy goods vehicle that is signalling to turn right, what should a driver do?
ABMW0350R

Stay behind until there is sufficient space to overtake it on the inside or until it has completed the turn.

Heavy goods vehicles need extra space on the road, and when they are turning the overhang of the vehicle may swing out into the path of overtaking or passing traffic. For that reason, it is a good idea to stay back and let the heavy goods vehicle complete its turn unless there is sufficient space to overtake safely.

When driving behind a bus that is signalling to turn left and there is oncoming traffic, what should a driver do?   ABMW0351R

Stay back and allow it to complete the turn.

Always allow a bus to complete a left-hand turn, because your field of view is restricted, and it could be dangerous to attempt overtaking it.

What might be described as a bus driver's 'blind spots'?   ABMW0352R

The areas to the front, sides and rear of the bus which the driver cannot see.

A blind spot is an area that a driver cannot see when looking forward or when looking in the mirrors. The bigger the vehicle, the bigger the blind spots, and you should keep this in mind if you are driving behind a truck or a bus. If you are driving behind a truck and you cannot see the truck's mirror, then the truck driver cannot see you.

Where are the blind spots on a truck (for its driver) that a driver in a car behind the truck needs to be aware of?   ABMW0353R

The areas to the front, sides and rear which the driver of the truck cannot see.

A blind spot is an area that a driver cannot see when looking forward or when looking in the mirrors. The bigger the vehicle, the bigger the blind spots, and you should keep this in mind if you are driving behind a truck or a bus. If you are driving behind a truck and you cannot see the truck's mirror, then the truck driver cannot see you.

Where are the blind spots that a driver needs to be aware of when towing a loaded trailer?   ABMW0354R

The area to the side and rear of the vehicle and of the trailer that the driver cannot see.

A blind spot is an area that a driver cannot see when looking forward or when looking in the mirrors. You should check your blindspots before changing direction or changing lane. The bigger the vehicle, the bigger the blind spots, and you should keep this in mind if you are driving behind a large vehicle, such as one towing a loaded trailer. In this situation, if you cannot see the towing vehicle's mirror, then the driver of that vehicle cannot see you.

What should a driver do when driving on a wide road behind a vehicle that has signalled to turn right ahead?   ABMW0355R

Overtake on the left-hand side and carry on.

You may overtake on the left when the driver in front has moved out and signalled their intent to turn right and you are going straight ahead – provided there is enough room to do so safely and your path will not be obstructed by the swing of a large vehicle turning right.

Overtaking and U-turns

The questions that follow deal with overtaking on the left and performing U-turns. Each of these manoeuvres can be done only in limited circumstances; they each require the driver to exercise judgement and skill.

When is it permissible to overtake another vehicle on the left-hand side?
When the vehicle in front is signalling to turn right. ABMW0356R

You may overtake on the left when the driver in front has moved out and signalled their intent to turn right and you are going straight ahead – provided there is enough room to do so safely and your path will not be obstructed by the swing of a large vehicle turning right.

What should a driver who wishes to perform a U-turn do?
Check ahead and behind for approaching traffic. ABMW0357R

If you want to do a U-turn you must first choose a place where it is safe and legal to do it. Check all around for other road users and do not impede their right of way. Complete the manoeuvre efficiently and safely.

What should a driver who wishes to perform a turnabout do? ABMW0358R
Check ahead and behind for oncoming traffic and turn briskly while still keeping a look out.

If you want to do a turnabout, you must first choose a place where it is safe and legal to do so. Check all around for other road users and do not impede their right of way. Complete the manoeuvre efficiently and safely.

1
2
3

The driver's mental state

Driving a motor vehicle requires concentration, perception, judgement and reaction. These can all be affected if your mental state is impaired by tiredness, by being under pressure, by anger or distress, by frustrating or confusing traffic conditions, or by alcohol or drugs. The questions in this section check that you understand these issues and know how to deal with them.

Tiredness

Tiredness – or fatigue – is one of the main causes of serious road collisions. When you're very tired, you are much less alert and have poorer physical coordination, and your reaction times are much slower. You will also find it more difficult to 'read the road' and take in direction signs, warning signs and other information as you drive. And you run the very grave risk of dozing off at the wheel, with potentially fatal consequences.

What should drivers do if they become drowsy while driving?
Stop, take a break including a short walk if possible. ABMW0359R

Driving when you are tired can be very dangerous, and tiredness is one of the main causes of serious road collisions. If you become drowsy while driving, stop in a safe place and take a short nap. Then get some fresh air and stretch your legs for a few minutes before setting off again. Taking a caffeine-based drink such as coffee may also help.

What should the driver do if they are driving and feel tired?
The driver should stop and take a break. ABMW0360R

Driving when you are tired can be very dangerous, and it may cause you to micro-sleep (or nod off momentarily). At 100km/h you travel at 28 metres a second, so if you micro-sleep for just 4 seconds you would travel over 100 metres without being in control of the vehicle. Never drive if you are fighting sleep.

Resisting pressure

There are so many things that can stress you when you are driving: heavy traffic, bad weather, road works, waiting at level crossings, other drivers' bad behaviour – all of these can build up frustration and make it difficult to stay calm and focus on arriving safely at your destination. Your own emotional state can also play a big part in how well you drive. If you are worried or upset, angry or depressed, it will probably show in your driving.

What should a driver do if they are behind schedule in reaching a destination at an appointed time?
ABMW0361R
Be patient and drive so as to arrive safely.

You should always drive at a speed that allows you to stop safely within the distance you can see to be clear. Being late for an appointment is no excuse for exceeding speed limits or for driving at an unsafe speed. Arrive alive.

1
2
3

What should a driver do if they do not want to travel as fast as the vehicle in front?

ABMW0362R

The driver should keep to the left and allow vehicles to overtake if they wish.

Always read the road ahead and be prepared to react to any traffic situation. You should not drive so slowly that your vehicle unnecessarily blocks other road users. If you want to allow a vehicle behind to overtake, you may pull into the hard shoulder briefly as long as no pedestrians or cyclists are using it and there are no junctions or entrances nearby.

What should a driver do if they wish to drive across a busy road and the traffic lights which normally control the junction are temporarily out of action?

ABMW0365R

Take good observation, wait for a clear break in the traffic and proceed to cross the road.

Always read the road ahead and be prepared to react to any traffic situation. In this case, do not proceed until it is clear and safe to do so. Do not assume that you have the right of way.

What should a driver do if they see a school bus stopped on the left-hand side of the road ahead?

ABMW0366R

Reduce speed and overtake with caution.

Always read the road and be prepared to react to any traffic situation – in this case, be aware of vulnerable road users such as school children boarding or alighting from school buses

What should the driver do when driving behind a vehicle that is going from side to side on the road in an unsafe manner?

ABMW0367R

The driver should stay well back until the road widens sufficiently to allow safe overtaking.

You should always be prepared to react to hazards ahead. If the vehicle in front is moving from side to side, it may indicate that the driver is not paying full attention or that their driving is impaired by drink, drugs or tiredness. Overtake such a vehicle only if you are sure it is safe to do so. If you think the vehicle is a risk to the public safety, you should report it to the Gardaí or to traffic watch lo-call 1890 205 805.

What should a driver do if a heavy goods vehicle in front has moved out to make a left turn ahead. ABMW0368R

Stay behind it and allow it to finish the turn.

Always read the road ahead and be prepared to react to any traffic situation. In this case, you should be aware that the heavy goods vehicle will need extra space to complete the left-hand turn and you should remain behind the vehicle until it has completed its turn.

What should a driver do if a bus in front has moved out to make a left-hand turn and there is oncoming traffic? ABMW0369R

Stay back and allow the bus to complete the turn.

Always read the road ahead and be prepared to react to any traffic situation. In this case, you should be aware that the bus will need extra space to make the turn. So you should not overtake it if by doing so you would cause oncoming traffic to alter speed or course. Remember, you should never overtake when approaching a junction.

1

2

3

What should a driver do if they see a truck reversing into a side entrance on the left-hand side of the road ahead? ABMW0370R

Stop and wait until the way is clear.

Always read the road ahead and be prepared to react to any traffic situation. You should be aware of the difficulties that drivers of large vehicles can have reversing into a side entrance. In this case, a large vehicle reversing could obstruct your view of the road ahead as you approach, and you should proceed only if you are sure the way ahead is clear.

What should a driver do if they wish to turn right at traffic lights while the green light is showing and there is oncoming traffic approaching?

Go forward towards the centre of the junction and wait for a suitable gap to appear in the oncoming traffic before making the turn. ABMW0371R

If you wish to turn right at a set of traffic lights, drive into the junction when you see a green light, taking care not to block any oncoming traffic. Then complete the turn when it is safe to do so.

When is it permitted to force oncoming traffic onto the hard shoulder on the opposite side of the road while overtaking?

ABMW0372R

It is not permitted to force oncoming traffic onto the hard shoulder while overtaking.

Overtaking in the manner described here is dangerous. You should overtake another vehicle only when it is safe to do so, both for you and for all other traffic. Before you overtake, make sure the road ahead is clear and that you have enough room to complete the overtaking manoeuvre and return to your own side of the road without forcing any other road user to alter speed or course.

Forcing oncoming traffic onto the hard shoulder on the opposite side of the road - is this safe driving?

ABMW0373R

No, this is dangerous driving.

1

2

3

Overtaking in the manner described here is dangerous. You should overtake another vehicle only when it is safe to do so, both for you and for all other traffic. Before you overtake, make sure the road ahead is clear and that you have enough room to complete the overtaking manoeuvre and return to your own side of the road without forcing any other road user to alter speed or course.

When meeting oncoming traffic on a national road, is it permitted to move into the hard shoulder to allow following traffic to overtake?

Yes, temporarily when the hard shoulder is clear and it is safe to drive there while the faster traffic overtakes.

ABMW0374R

On national roads, the hard shoulder is normally for the use of pedestrians and cyclists only. If you want to allow a vehicle behind to overtake, you may pull into the hard shoulder briefly as long as no pedestrians or cyclists are using it and there are no junctions or entrances nearby. In the case of motorways, however, you must not drive on the hard shoulder, except in an emergency.

When driving on a national road is it permitted to drive on the hard shoulder in order to allow faster-moving traffic to overtake.

Yes, temporarily when the hard shoulder is clear and it is safe to drive there while the traffic is overtaking.

ABMW0375R

On national roads, the hard shoulder is normally for the use of pedestrians and cyclists only. If you want to allow a vehicle behind to overtake, you may pull into the hard shoulder briefly as long as no pedestrians or cyclists are using it and there are no junctions or entrances nearby. In the case of motorways, however, you must not drive on the hard shoulder, except in an emergency.

What action should a driver take in a queue of traffic controlled by traffic lights?
ABMW0376R

A driver should always maintain their position in the queue.

Always read the road ahead and be prepared to react to any traffic situation. From time to time you may have to queue in traffic. In this situation, you should try to remain patient and considerate of other road users. Jumping the queue is inconsiderate, it could be dangerous , and may it could even provoke a road rage incident or cause a collision.

What should the driver do when driving a vehicle they are not familiar with?
ABMW0377R

Drive initially with extra care and at a lower speed than normal.

You should know where to find and how to operate all the controls on your vehicle, including all of its safety features and warning lamps. When you are driving, you need to be able to concentrate on what's happening around you and operating the vehicle controls should be second nature to you. When you sit into the driver's seat of a vehicle you are not familiar with, you should do a thorough 'cockpit drill' before you move off.

What should drivers do if they approach road works and there is earth-moving machinery moving about?
ABMW0378R

Reduce speed as there may be loose gravel or mud on the road.

Where earth-moving machinery is working, there are likely to be mud and gravel deposits on the road. Also the noise of such machines might make it hard for road workers to hear the approaching traffic. When you come across earth-moving machinery, slow down and proceed with extreme caution.

Subject to the speed limit, what is the 'safest' speed to drive at?
The speed that will enable the driver to stop the vehicle within the distance ahead that they can see to be clear.
ABMW0379

You should always drive at a speed that allows you to stop within the distance ahead that you can see to be clear. If you don't think you could safely bring the vehicle to a stop within the range of what you can see, then you're driving too fast – slow down.

1

2

3

Keeping full attention on the road

When you are driving you need to take in a great deal of information – about other traffic, road conditions, direction and warning signs, and so on. Just dealing with that amount of information is quite enough, and you don't need to add to the load by letting yourself be distracted. When you are distracted, your reactions are slower and your judgement is not as good. Remember that it is an offence to drive 'without due care and attention'.

When driving along and wishing to use a hand- held mobile phone, what should a driver do?
ABMW0380R

Stop at a safe location before using the phone.

It is an offence and very unsafe to use a hand-held mobile phone while driving a vehicle or riding a motorbike. It is unsafe because it prevents you from concentrating fully on your driving. Using a hands-free phone kit is not illegal, but in some circumstances it could be a dangerous distraction, and you could be prosecuted for dangerous driving, careless driving or driving without due care and attention.

When stopped at traffic lights and the green light comes on, what should a driver do?
ABMW0381R

Check that other road users have cleared the junction and move off with care.

When stopped at traffic lights and the green light comes on, you should check to ensure the way is clear and proceed only if it is safe to do so.

Patience and courtesy

Aggressive and impatient behaviour can very easily turn into 'road rage', where people who are normally civil and courteous lose self-control and act very irresponsibly. Don't allow yourself to be provoked by other drivers' bad behaviour. Let such drivers go ahead – you will be safer if you are not in their vicinity.

Good drivers stay patient, courteous and tolerant at all times and don't respond to provocation – they know that they'll get there just as quickly if they ignore such actions.

What should a driver do if another vehicle blocks their right of way at a junction?

Be patient. ABMW0382R

You should always try to show restraint. It is important to understand that the right of way is not an absolute right of way, and you must always proceed with caution and with regard for other road users.

1

2

3

A driver who is about to undertake a journey is upset or angry. What should they do?

Not drive until they are calm. ABMW0383R

If you drive when you are angry or upset, you are more likely to be involved in a collision, and more likely to react to other drivers' bad behaviour. Take the time to calm down and compose yourself before you set out on a journey.

When being overtaken and there is oncoming traffic, what should a driver do? ABMW0384R

Reduce speed and allow the overtaking vehicle to return the left side of the road after completing the overtaking manoeuvre.

When you are being overtaken and there are oncoming vehicles, you should show consideration for all the other traffic and slow down to allow the overtaking vehicle to move in front of you to avoid the risk of a collision.

When in a hurry and another vehicle cuts in front, what should a driver do?

ABMW0385R

Be patient and not retaliate.

If another driver behaves badly, you should try not let it annoy you – show restraint and don't react. Road rage only increases the risk of a collision.

What should a driver do when they get a puncture while driving?

ABMW0386R

Stop at a safe place and change the tyre.

If you get a puncture while driving, find a suitable and safe place to stop and change the wheel. If you can't find a suitable place immediately, drive slowly (with your hazard warning lights turned on) to avoid further damage to the tyre or rim until a safe place is found.

What should a driver do when they want to change to the lane on the right in which there is other traffic?

ABMW0387R

Use the mirror, signal and move into the right-hand lane when a suitable gap appears in the traffic in that lane.

Any time you change lanes, you should use the Mirror–Signal–Mirror (blind spots)–Manoeuvre routine.

Check your mirrors, signal your intention, check your mirrors again (and your blind spots), and when a suitable gap becomes available manoeuvre the vehicle into the next lane, giving way to traffic already in that lane.

1

2

3

Alcohol and drugs

Alcohol and many other drugs seriously impair your ability to drive safely. The questions in this section check that you fully understand this issue and know how to comply with the law in this respect.

What effect does alcohol have on driver behaviour?
It slows down a driver's reactions.   ABMW0388R

Alcohol is a major factor in collisions that lead to death and injury. Even small amounts of alcohol affect your judgement, your concentration and your ability to react to hazards. A driver should never ever drink and drive.

What effect does drinking alcohol have on a driver?
It makes the driver drowsy.   ABMW0389R

Alcohol is a major factor in collisions that lead to death and injury. Even small amounts of alcohol affect your judgement, your concentration and your ability to react to hazards. A driver should never ever drink and drive.

If a motorist or a motorcyclist is taking medication which may affect their driving, what should they do?
ABMW0390R

Seek medical advice in relation to driving.

Some medication can affect a driver's ability to drive safely. If you are on medication of any kind, you should ask your doctor or pharmacist to tell you if it is safe to drive while taking it. Read the patient information leaflet supplied with the medication.

1

2

3

According to the pre-crash Report which gender was more likely to drink and drive and be involved in a fatal collision?

RSA00037A

Males

The pre-crash Report found that more male than female drivers drink and drive and are involved in a fatal collision in Ireland. This means you need to be careful who you accept a lift from – can you be certain that your friend has not been drinking before they met up with you?

Be sensible and say no to a lift if you suspect your friend has been drinking and plans to drive. If in doubt, make other arrangements for getting home.

According to the pre-crash Report what type of vehicle were the majority of people driving when they had consumed alcohol and caused a fatal collision?

RSA00038A

Private car

The pre-crash Report found that more private car drivers take alcohol than drivers of any other type of vehicle before being involved in a crash. This means that if you arrange a lift home in a car, after socialising where drink was available, you are more likely to have a driver who has taken alcohol. That means you cannot take your safety for granted. Do what you can to protect yourself and other friends – including the driver.

According to the pre-crash Report what type of fatal collision was a person more likely to be involved in when drink driving?

Single-vehicle collision

RSA00039A

The pre-crash Report found that the most common type of crash where alcohol is a factor is a single vehicle collision.

According to the pre-crash Report which days of the week were people more likely to drink and drive and cause a fatal collision?

Saturday and Sunday

RSA00040A

The pre-crash Report found that more alcohol related collisions occur on Saturday and Sunday compared to other days of the week.

According to pre-crash Report how did the use of alcohol affect a person's decision to use a seatbelt?

RSA00041A

Drivers and passengers were less likely to wear a seatbelt.

The pre-crash Report found that fewer drivers and passengers wore a seatbelt, in a car, after being drinking compared to drivers and passengers who had not been drinking. The evidence is that alcohol affects your judgment. This, combined with the fact that a driver is more likely to be distracted in this state, means a dangerous situation can develop quickly.

What is the minimum blood alcohol concentration (BAC) level at which a learner or a novice driver is committing an offence?

RSA00042A

20mg

The law sets different drink driving limits according to various categories of driver, with Blood Alcohol Concentration levels ranging from 20mg to 80mg. Learner or novice drivers are subject to the lowest drink driving limit.

What is the maximum disqualification period imposed in court where the learner driver has a blood alcohol concentration (BAC) level in excess of 80 mg?

RSA00049A

Six years

When a learner driver is tested and has a Blood Alcohol Concentration level of over 80mg they face a driving ban of up to six years.

So, think about that for a moment. How much do you depend on your car? Do you drive to work? Do family members depend on you for lifts?

This can be all affected by you having a drink and then getting behind the wheel of a car.

According to the pre-crash Report which age group had the highest number of drivers causing fatal collisions where alcohol was a factor?

RSA00043A

16-24 years

The pre-crash Report found that drivers aged 16-24 years were more likely to drink and drive and cause a fatal collision. However, drinking and driving at any age is dangerous.

1

2

3

According to the pre-crash Report how many people were killed by a driver who had consumed alcohol?

RSA00044A

More than 251

The pre-crash Report found that between 2008 and 2012, at least 286 people were killed on our roads as a result of a driver who had consumed alcohol. Sadly, drivers still drink and drive. You can decide yourself or, better still, with your friends to never drink and drive. You can also decide to be careful about not distracting the driver while they are driving. It sounds simple – everyone should be able to do it. Discuss the issue and the consequences of drink driving when you are not out drinking. You owe it to yourselves, your friends and your families.

A driver is automatically disqualified from driving for how long if, on a first offence, they refused to provide a member of An Garda Síochána with a sample of blood, urine or breath?

RSA00045A

4 years

Drivers who refuse to provide a Garda with a breath, blood or urine sample can, for a first offence, be disqualified from driving for four years. But you don't need to be afraid of providing a sample if you have not been drinking. Please take time to consider the effect on your life and on your friends and family if you are banned from driving for any length of time.

Which of the following is a possible consequence for a learner driver if they drive after drinking as little as just one unit of alcohol?

A three month disqualification from driving

RSA00046A

Even if you are within the legal limit for drinking, your driving will be affected. The safest approach is to never drink and drive. In some cases, one drink may push a learner driver over the reduced Blood Alcohol Concentration (BAC) level and lead to a three month disqualification from driving.

According to the pre-crash Report out of 867 fatal collisions how many had alcohol as a contributory factor?

RSA00056A

251-350

Drink driving is a killer behaviour. 330 collisions involved a driver, cyclist, motorcyclists or pedestrian who had consumed alcohol. The pre-crash Report found that the most common collision type – where alcohol is a factor – is a single vehicle collision.

According to the pre-crash Report what age group had the highest number of passenger deaths in collisions where alcohol was a factor?

17-24 years

RSA00048A

The pre-crash Report found that passengers in the 17-24 age group are at the highest risk of being killed in a collision involving alcohol. All drinking and driving is dangerous but this age group is most likely to be at risk.

Be sensible and say no to a lift if you suspect your friend has been drinking and plans to drive. If in doubt make other arrangements for getting home.

According to the pre-crash Report how many passengers were killed in a collision where alcohol was a known factor?

71 – 90

RSA00055A

The pre-crash Report found that 83 passengers were killed in an alcohol related collision where a driver or motorcyclist had been drinking between 2008 and 2012. In addition, passengers who have been drinking may contribute to crashes, sometimes distracting the driver. Safe and socially responsible road use goes beyond the drivers themselves. If you want to stay safe, you must take responsibility for your own actions, especially as to how they might affect drivers and other road users.

1

2

3

According to the pre-crash Report what percentage of the 169 drivers killed in an alcohol related collision had consumed alcohol?

92%

RSA00050A

The figures speak for themselves; The pre-crash Report found that 9 out of 10 drink drivers who were killed in alcohol related collisions had consumed alcohol prior to the fatal collision. Drivers are affected by drinking even small amounts of alcohol. Alcohol affects your judgement, vision, co-ordination and reaction time, which in turn lead to serious driving errors.

According to the pre-crash Report how many pedestrians were killed where alcohol consumption by the pedestrian was a factor?

RSA00051A

41 = 90

Alcohol affects everybody who takes it. The pre-crash Report found that more than 81 pedestrians killed during 2008-2012 had consumed alcohol. This shows us that no matter what kind of road user you are, you need to take care and avoid using the roads when you have been drinking.

According to the pre-crash Report in how many fatal collisions was alcohol a contributory factor?

RSA00053A

4 out of 10

The pre-crash Report found that the number of fatal collisions where alcohol was a factor was about 4 out of every 10. Drink driving is a killer behaviour. Drivers take the risk despite the high death rates. The RSA believes that some drivers are not considering the consequences. Otherwise, they would never ever drink and drive. Alcohol affects your judgment. Even one drink, where you may still be below the legal limit, will alter your behaviour. There is no safe limit.

During what time periods can a driver be tested for drugs at a road side checkpoint?

RSA01045

Anytime of day or night.

The law allows for a driver to be tested at any time for drugs after a crash, if you have commited a driving offence or if a Garda forms the opion that you have consumed an intoxicant such as alcohol or certian drugs. The time of days has no bearing on whan test can take place and it is an offence to refuse to perform impariment tests.

Overtaking and driving when weather or road conditions are hazardous

Before overtaking a slower-moving vehicle, ask yourself whether it is necessary to do so, whether it is legal, and, above all, whether it is safe. When passing parked vehicles, leave enough room for the door of the parked vehicle to open. And when driving on icy roads, make sure that you leave enough stopping distance between your vehicle and the vehicle in front.

What effect does a wet road surface have on a vehicle's braking ability?
Generally, it doubles the normal braking distance required on a dry surface. ABMW0392R

When it is wet, your tyres do not grip the road surface as well as when it is dry and your stopping distance is increased. For these reasons you should slow down during or after rain and keep a greater distance from the vehicle in front.

After overtaking another vehicle, what should a driver do? ABMW0394R
Gradually move back into the left when the vehicle has been overtaken.

After overtaking, check your mirrors, signal and return to your normal lane position as soon as it is safe. Take a smooth easy line and don't cut in sharply.

What could happen if a driver cuts in too soon when overtaking another vehicle? ABMW0395A
The vehicles could collide.

When overtaking make sure the road ahead is clear so you have enough distance to overtake and get back to your own side of the road without forcing any other road user to move to avoid you. When you are well past, check the mirror, signal and gradually move in making sure not to cut across the vehilce you have passed.

What should a driver do when overtaking parked vehicles?
Allow sufficient clearance when passing. ABMW0396R

When you are passing a parked vehicle, move into the correct position in good time and leave plenty of clearance room between your vehicle and the parked vehicle – just in case someone opens the door in front of you.

What stopping distance should a driver allow when they suspect that the road might be icy? ABMW0397R
Up to ten times the normal distance.

When driving in snow or icy conditions a driver should allow a greater distance from the vehicle in front as stopping distances can be increased by up to ten times the normal.

What clearance should drivers normally allow for parked vehicles?
A door width. ABMW0398R

When you are passing a parked vehicle, move into the correct position in good time and leave plenty of clearance room between your vehicle and the parked vehicle – just in case someone opens the door in front of you.

Why does it take longer to stop the vehicle on a wet road?
The tyres have less road grip than in dry weather. ABMW0399A

Wet or greasy roads reduce the grip of your tyres on the road and is a possible source of skidding

Roadholding

Your ability to control your vehicle and to stop it safely and effectively depends to a large extent on the quality of your tyres, the road surface and the contact between them. The tyres' grip on the road can be reduced or even eliminated by water, oil, ice, wet leaves, or loose chippings. You need to be aware of this fact, and reduce speed if you are driving in these conditions.

1

2

3

What is the effect on driving if there is a film of water between the vehicle's tyres and the road surface?
Steering and braking will be less effective. ABMW0400R

On a wet road, a film of water can build up between the tyres and the road surface. This is called 'aquaplaning' and it has the effect of reducing the grip of the tyres on the road.

What should a driver do if they encounter loose chippings on a road?
Slow down and allow extra clearance to all traffic until they have gone past the area with the loose chippings. ABMW0401R

Where there are loose chippings on the road, you should slow down and leave extra room (or clearance) between your vehicle and other traffic. This will also give you more time to stop if you need to, and it will help to reduce the amount of chippings your vehicle throws up against other vehicles.

What effect does spilt diesel have on a road? ABMW0402RA
It makes the road more slippery.

Diesel spilt on the road can make the road surface extremely slippery, particularly if the road is wet.

What should a driver do when driving in slippery road conditions?

Drive at lower speeds and use gentle acceleration and braking. ABMW0403R

When driving in slippery road conditions, you should be particularly smooth and gradual in the way you accelerate and brake. This will help you avoid skidding or slipping.

What should a driver do when travelling downhill on snow or ice?

Use an appropriate lower gear and brake gently to reduce speed. ABMW0404R

When travelling downhill in snow or ice, you should select a lower gear to take advantage of engine braking and use the brakes very gently when you need to.

Maintaining a safe distance from the vehicle in front

Never drive too close to the vehicle in front of you. The faster the traffic is moving, the greater the distance you should allow. The distance it will take you to stop in an emergency depends on many things, including how alert you are, the type and condition of the road surface, and the condition of your brakes and tyres. The questions in this section check that you understand the need to keep your distance, and that you know how to do so.

How does driving at high speed affect a vehicle's road holding?

The road holding ability of the vehicle is reduced. ABMW0405R

Driving at high speed is a factor that affects road holding. At higher speeds the airflow under a vehicle reduces tyre grip on the road and when you are approaching a bend or corner, the momentum of the vehicle makes it more difficult to change direction.

What is the recommended minimum stopping distance for a car travelling at 50Km/h on a dry road? ABMW0406RA

25 metres.

The total minimum stopping distance of your vehicle depends on four things; your perception time, your reaction time, your vehicle reaction time and you vehicle braking capability. The recommend minimum stopping distance of a car driving at 50km/h under dry conditions is 25 metres.

What is the recommended minimum stopping distance for a car travelling at 50km/h on a wet road?

ABMW0407RA

36 metres.

The total minimum stopping distance of your vehicle depends on four things; your perception time, your reaction time, your vehicle reaction time and you vehicle braking capability. The recommend minimum stopping distance of a car driving at 50km/h under wet conditions is 36 metres.

What is the recommended minimum stopping distance for a car travelling at 100km/h on a dry road?

ABMW0408RA

70 metres.

The total minimum stopping distance of your vehicle depends on four things; your perception time, your reaction time, your vehicle reaction time and you vehicle braking capability. The recommend minimum stopping distance of a car driving at 100km/h under dry conditions is 70 metres.

What is the recommended minimum stopping distance for a car travelling at 100km/h on a wet road?

ABMW0409RA

121 metres.

The total minimum stopping distance of your vehicle depends on four things; your perception time, your reaction time, your vehicle reaction time and you vehicle braking capability. The recommend minimum stopping distance of a car driving at 100km/h under wet conditions is 121 metres.

What is the minimum safe distance to leave between vehicles travelling at 100Km/h on a dry road?

62 metres.

ABMW0413R

The figure of 62 metres is based on the two-second rule. If you follow the two-second rule, you will leave approximately 1 metre between you and the vehicle in front for every 1.6 km/h of your speed.

ABMW0425R

What is a likely consequence of sudden braking?

The vehicle could be hit from behind.

As well as reading the road ahead, you should also be aware of traffic coming behind you. This will help you react correctly in a situation where you need to brake suddenly.

1

2

3

Which of the following affects the braking distance of a vehicle?

The speed and weight of the vehicle.

ABMW0426R

The overall stopping distance of your vehicle depends on its speed and weight – faster and heavier vehicles require greater stopping distances.

In dry weather how might a driver judge what is a safe following distance to vehicle in front?

ABMW0427R

By allowing at least two seconds to elapse between the vehicle in front and the driver's own vehicle passing a fixed point.

You should maintain a gap of at least two seconds from the vehicle in front – that's the two-second rule.

In wet weather how might a driver judge what is a safe following distance from the vehicle in front?

ABMW0428R

By allowing at least four seconds to elapse between the vehicle in front and the driver's own vehicle passing a fixed point.

In wet conditions you should maintain a gap of at least four seconds from the vehicle in front – twice as long as in dry conditions.

What phrase is recommended for drivers to help them determine a 'safe headway' distance from the vehicle in front on a dry road?

ABMW0429RA

"Only a fool breaks the two second rule."

You should maintain a gap of least two seconds from the vehicle in front – that's the two-second rule.

What effect does carrying a load have on a vehicle's braking ability?

It increases the distance required to stop.

ABMW0430R

When driving a vehicle which is carrying a load, the driver should be aware that the forces acting on the load under braking will increase the distance required to stop.

What effect does towing a loaded trailer have on stopping ability?

It significantly increases stopping distance.

ABMW0434R

If you are towing a loaded trailer, you need to be aware that your braking distance could be considerably greater, depending on the weight and size of the trailer.

Driving when visibility is reduced

When your visibility is reduced, such as in rain, snow or fog, you must modify your driving behaviour. The questions in this section check that you understand this issue and can take appropriate action when necessary.

1

2

3

What should a driver do when driving in dense fog?
Drive with dipped headlights and fog lights.   ABMW0435R

In dense fog you should use dipped headlights and fog lights (where fitted). Sidelights are not strong enough in fog, and full headlights can reflect off the fog and make it harder to see where you are going.

What should a driver do when driving in dense fog?
Reduce speed and use dipped headlights.   ABMW0436R

In dense fog you should reduce your speed and use dipped headlights and fog lights (where fitted). Sidelights are not strong enough in fog, and full headlights can reflect off the fog and make it harder to see where you are going.

Driving at night

1

2

3

Driving at night is considerably more challenging than driving during the day. You need to drive more slowly to take account of the reduced visibility, and you need to use your lights to make sure that you can be seen by other road users and that you can see the road ahead.

When driving at night the full headlights should enable the driver to see for a distance of how many metres?   ABMW0437R
100 metres.

At night in good driving conditions the full headlights of a car will typically let you see 100 metres ahead. So, you should travel at a speed that allows you to stop within that distance.

When driving at night the dipped headlights should enable the driver to see for a distance of how many metres?   ABMW0438R
30 metres.

When driving at night in good driving conditions the dipped headlights of a car will typically let you see 30 metres ahead. So, you should travel at a speed that allows you to stop in that distance.

What effect could incorrectly adjusted headlights have?

Oncoming road users could be dazzled. ABMW0439R

You are responsible for making sure that your vehicle is roadworthy and that its headlights are adjusted correctly. If the headlights are out of line they are less effective and may dazzle oncoming traffic, even when dipped.

When driving at night, when must a driver dip the vehicle's full headlights? ABMW0440R

When meeting or driving behind other traffic.

When driving at night you should dip your headlights when you meet oncoming vehicles so that you do not dazzle them. And you should also dip your headlights when you are driving behind another vehicle so the driver is not dazzled by your lights in their mirror.

When driving at night and blinded by the lights of an oncoming vehicle, what should a driver do? ABMW0441R

Look away and slow down and stop if necessary.

If you are dazzled by the lights of an oncoming vehicle, look towards the verge until the vehicle has passed. Slow down and stop if necessary.

A driver has been driving regularly in daylight and must now undertake a journey at night. What should the driver do? ABMW0442R

Drive at a slower speed than in the day as visibility is reduced at night.

If you are not very used to driving at night time, it can take quite a while to adjust to conditions at night. For that reason, you might need to drive slower until you get used to the reduced visibility at night.

1
2
3

What should a driver do when driving at night?

ABMW0443R

Drive at a speed that enables the driver to stop within the distance ahead that they can see to be clear.

When driving at night in good driving conditions the full headlights of a car will typically let you see 100 metres ahead. So, you should travel at a speed that allows you to stop in that distance.

When driving at night, what is the safest approach for a driver to adopt?

Drive at a speed that enables the driver to stop within the distance ahead that they can see to be clear.

ABMW0444R

When driving at night in good driving conditions the dipped headlights of a car will typically let you see 30 metres ahead. So, you should travel at a speed that allows you to stop in that distance.

When meeting an oncoming vehicle at night, what should a driver do?

Not look directly at the oncoming vehicle's lights.

ABMW0445R

If you are dazzled by the lights of an oncoming vehicle, look towards the verge until the vehicle has passed and /or slow down and stop if necessary.

When may a driver use full headlights when driving at night?

When there is no oncoming traffic.

ABMW0446R

You should use full headlights when driving at night in unlit rural areas – this will enable you to see as far ahead as possible. Make sure, however, that your lights do not dazzle or inconvenience other road users in any way.

What lights should a driver have on when driving close behind other traffic at night?

Dipped headlights.

ABMW0447R

You should dip your headlights when you are driving behind another vehicle so the driver is not dazzled by your lights in their mirror.

When must a driver use dipped headlights?

ABMW0448R

When meeting or driving behind other traffic.

When driving at night you should dip your headlights when meeting or following traffic so as not to dazzle or blind other drivers.

When driving late at night what should a driver be aware of?

ABMW0449R

That there is a danger of falling asleep.

Driving when you are tired can be very dangerous, and tiredness is one of the main causes of serious road collisions. If you become drowsy while driving, stop in a safe place and take a short nap. Then get some fresh air and stretch your legs for a few minutes before setting off again. Taking a caffeine-based drink such as coffee may also help.

What should a driver do if dazzled by the lights of an oncoming vehicle at night?

ABMW0450R

Do not look directly at the lights.

If you are dazzled by the lights of an oncoming vehicle, look towards the verge until the vehicle has passed and /or slow down and stop if necessary.

When driving at night, a single headlight approaches from ahead. What should a driver do?

ABMW0451R

Be aware it may be a four-wheeled vehicle.

When you see a single oncoming headlight at night, you need to be aware that it might not be a motorcycle – it could be a car or a van with a broken headlight.

1
2
3

Driving on slippery roads

Driving on a road that is covered with water, oil, ice, wet leaves or loose chippings is particularly dangerous, because your vehicle's tyres have greatly reduced 'grip' on the road surface and you may skid and lose control of the vehicle. The questions in this section check that you understand this danger and know how to respond.

How might a driver know if there is black ice on the road?

ABMW0452R

There will be a decrease in road noise in the vehicle.

One of the signs that you might be driving on black ice is a sudden decrease in the level of road noise. This is due to the lack of grip between the tyres and the road.

What should a driver do if there is black ice on the road?

ABMW0453R

Avoid harsh braking, steering and acceleration.

If you suspect you are driving on black ice, you should avoid harsh braking, steering and acceleration. This will help reduce the risk of skidding.

When is black ice likely to occur on the road?

ABMW0454R

In cold weather after rain.

Black ice occurs when moisture freezes on a very cold surface. Exposed roads and bridges can have black ice when other sections of the same road may be clear. Black ice is virtually invisible, and so presents a particular hazard for motorcyclists and drivers. In wintry conditions, if you notice a reduction in tyre noise or if the steering becomes lighter, you should suspect that there may be black ice on the road.

What is the safest practice when driving on icy roads?

ABMW0455R

Drive at a slower speed than usual using gentle acceleration and braking.

When driving on icy roads you should avoid harsh braking, steering and acceleration. This will help reduce the risk of skidding.

When driving a vehicle, what effect could icy roads have?

ABMW0456R

The vehicle could skid more easily than normal.

Icy roads can have a dramatic effect on the way a vehicle handles, and there can be an increased risk of skidding. When driving on icy roads you should avoid harsh braking, steering and acceleration. This will help reduce the risk of skidding.

How might a driver know if there is black ice on the road?
Steering will seem lighter. ABMW15

One of the signs that that you might be driving on black ice is that the steering will seem lighter than normal. This is due to the lack of grip between the tyres and the road.

What should a driver do when driving in slippery road conditions?
Use gentle acceleration and braking. ABMW0457R

Your tyres have less grip on the road when it is wet or icy. Slow down in slippery conditions, and keep a greater distance from the vehicle in front.

How should a driver negotiate a bend when the road is slippery?
Drive slowly and smoothly. ABMW0458R

Be extra careful when negotiating bends in slippery conditions. Slow down gently on the approach, select the appropriate gear for the speed of the vehicle and use gentle steering and acceleration to drive around the bend. Avoid braking in the bend as this may cause the vehicle to become unstable and cause a skid.

Apart from the risk of skidding, what danger may arise when driving in snow?
ABMW0459R

Road signs and road markings may become obscured.

Road signs and road markings may become obscured by snow. If this happens you may have difficulty reading regulatory, warning and information signs. This is the main reason why these signs are different shapes. Drivers should pay particular attention when travelling in these conditions.

What should a driver do when driving in heavy rain?
Be on the alert for sliding or 'aquaplaning'. ABMW0460R

On a wet road, a film of water can build up between the tyres and the road surface. This is called 'aquaplaning ' and it has the effect of reducing the grip of the tyres on the road, and this affects your steering and braking. For these reasons you should slow down during and after rain and keep a greater distance from the vehicle in front.

1
2
3

What is the danger in driving with badly worn tyres at high speed on wet roads? ABMW0461R

Control of the vehicle is reduced because it is gliding on a film of water.

Worn tyres will reduce a vehicle's grip on the road. This becomes more noticeable on wet roads. As tyres become worn their ability to channel away the water between the tyre and the road diminishes. The minimum legal tread depth for motorcycles is 1mm and 1.6mm for other vehicles. However tyres should be replaced before they become this worn.

What should a driver do when they encounter mud on the road? ABMW0462R

Reduce speed and be aware of the farm or works vehicles on the road.

Where there is mud on the road you should slow down and be aware that there is a danger of skidding. Your stopping distance will also be greater where there is mud on the road.

What should a driver be aware of when crossing tram lines at an angle?

Be aware that tyre grip is reduced on the lines. ABMW0463R

Tyre grip may be reduced when you cross tram lines, especially in icy or wet conditions. As you approach tram lines, you should slow down, avoid harsh acceleration or sudden braking, and keep a greater distance from the vehicle in front . Be extra careful when there are vulnerable road users such as pedestrians and cyclists using the crossing.

What should a driver be aware of when crossing road markings such as lines or arrows? ABMW0464R

Tyre grip is reduced.

Tyre grip is reduced when you are crossing road markings such as arrows and lines, and you should be extra careful when driving over these in wet conditions.

Driving on flooded roads

When you have driven through a large puddle or flooded area, you should test your brakes to make sure that they have not been affected by the water. If they have been affected (and if it is safe to do so), press gently on the brake pedal as you are driving until the brakes dry out and return to normal.

What should a driver do after passing trough a flooded section of road?
Apply the brake pedal lightly at slow speed for a short distance to dry the
brakes. ABMW0465R

When you drive through a flooded section of road, your brakes may become less effective. If this happens, test your brakes to ensure that they have not been affected by the water check in your mirrors before you do this. If they have been affected (and this is more than likely just temporary), press gently on the brake pedal as you are driving until they dry out and return to normal.

How does wet weather affect a vehicle's engine performance?
It has no effect on power output. ABMW0466R

Wet weather does not affect the performance of the vehicle's engine. It does, however, affect the vehicle's road holding and braking distances. It can also affect a driver's observations.

What should a driver do where a section of road ahead has a shallow flooded area.
ABMW0467R
Reduce speed and use a lower gear.

When you approach a stretch of road with shallow flooding, you should reduce your speed and assess the area for any danger. As you drive through surface water, you should think of pedestrians and cyclists and try not to splash them as you pass.

1

2

3

Roadworks

The National Roads Authority and local authorities around the country are continually working to provide a safe, efficient road network and to maintain the quality of road surfaces. Roadworks include the construction of new roads, emergency repairs, routine maintenance of fences and barriers, trimming hedgerows, clearing litter, cutting grass verges, and so on.

When you come across roadworks of any kind, you need to drive with extra care, for your own safety, the safety of other road users and the safety of the road workers.

What should a driver do when they approach roadworks warning signs?
Reduce speed and be prepared to stop for works vehicles or a flagman. ABMW0468R

You should always approach roadworks with caution as there are many possible hazards to deal with – including road workers, works vehicles, uneven road surfaces and temporary traffic controls.

What should a driver be aware of when driving through a section of road where roadworks are ongoing?
ABMW0469R

That the surface may be slippery due to mud or loose chippings.

When you are travelling through a section of roadworks, you need to be extra careful, as the road surface may be uneven or slippery or there may be loose chippings, all of which can affect road holding.

Driving on different types of road

Different types of road require you to drive in different ways, impose different restrictions on what you must or must not do, and present different things that you must look out for. The questions in this section deal with a variety of road types and the challenges they present, and check that you know how to behave when driving on them.

1
2
3

One-way streets

Driving on a one-way street can be confusing. Your inclination may be to always adopt a position to the left of the street, as would be appropriate if it were a two-way street. However, if you wish to turn right off the street, you should take up a position to the right.

When driving on a one-way street and wishing to turn right, what should a driver do?
ABMW0470R

Drive close to the right-hand side of the road.

When driving on a one-way street, you should normally keep to the left. When you want to turn right you should check your mirrors, signal right and manoeuvre into the right-hand side when it is safe to do so. Then complete the turn into the appropriate lane of the street you are entering.

When driving on a one-way street and wishing to turn right up ahead, what should a driver do?
ABMW0471R

Move to the right- hand side in good time.

When driving on a one-way street, you should normally keep to the left. When you want to turn right you should check your mirrors, signal right and manoeuvre into the right-hand side when it is safe to do so. Then complete the turn into the appropriate lane of the street you are entering.

Bus lanes

There are two types of bus lane: 'with-flow' bus lanes and 'contra-flow' bus lanes, and the rules governing what vehicles may use them are different. In addition, a bus lane may be operational only at certain times of the day, as specified on the plate accompanying the bus lane sign.

When a driver wants to turn left into a property and there is a bus lane on the left, what should the driver do?
ABMW0472R

Watch out for cyclists, taxis and buses which may be using the bus lane.

If you need to cross a bus lane on your left in order to enter a property, you should take extra care that there are no buses, taxis or cyclists in the bus lane. Check your mirrors, signal and turn into the property when it is safe to do so.

What traffic may use a contra-flow bus lane?
ABMW0474

Buses on a scheduled service

A bus lane is a special lane for the use of buses. Taxis and cyclists may use some bus lanes. A contra-flow bus lane is one that runs in the opposite direction to traffic beside it. Only buses on a scheduled service may use a contra-flow bus lane.

What traffic may use a with-flow bus lane during the specific times?
ABMW0475R

Buses, taxis and cyclists.

A bus lane is a special lane for the use of buses. A 'with-flow' bus lane is one that runs in the same direction as the traffic beside it. Taxis and cyclists may also use with-flow bus lanes. Other traffic may use them outside the hours posted on the accompanying plate.

Dual carriageways

The questions in this section deal with entering, crossing and driving along dual carriageways. Traffic on these roads is generally faster that on other roads, so you need to know how to act appropriately without undue hesitation.

When driving along a dual carriageway, what lane position should a driver be in?
ABMW0477R

In the left-hand lane unless the driver wishes to overtake or turn right.

You must normally drive in the left-hand lane of a dual carriageway, except when overtaking or turning right a short distance ahead.

1
2
3

'2-plus-1' roads

'2-plus-1' roads provide two lanes in one direction and one lane in the opposite direction. On the two-lane side, it is generally safe to overtake. Approximately every two kilometres, the two-lane side is replaced by one lane and the one-lane side opens out into two lanes. The questions in this section check that you understand how to drive on such roads.

What does a 2-plus-1 road have?
ABMW0480R

Two non-motorway lanes in one direction and one non-motorway lane in the opposite direction.

A 2-plus-1 road consists of two lanes in one direction of travel and one lane in the other direction. The two-lane section allows for safe overtaking and alternates with a one-lane section roughly every 2 kilometres.

On a 2-plus-1 road, where must a driver only turn right?
ABMW0481R

At controlled junctions.

A 2-plus-1 road consists of two lanes in one direction of travel and one lane in the other direction. There may be safety barriers separating the two directions of traffic, so in this situation you may turn right only at junctions.

What does a 2-plus-1 road have?
ABMW0482R

Two lanes of traffic in one direction and one in the opposite direction.

A 2-plus-1 road consists of two lanes in one direction of travel and one lane in the other direction. The two-lane section allows for safe overtaking and alternates with a one-lane section roughly every 2 kilometres.

Where may a driver overtake on a 2-plus-1 road?
ABMW0483R

In the two-lane stretch.

A 2-plus-1 road consists of two lanes in one direction of travel and one lane in the other direction. When you need to overtake, you should wait until you reach the 2-lane section which occurs approximately every 2 kilometres.

Motorways

Driving on a motorway requires concentration and discipline. You need to know exactly how to behave when entering and leaving a motorway, how to drive on it, and what to expect from other drivers while on it. Although you are not permitted to drive on a motorway while holding a learner permit, the questions in this section check that you know and understand the issues involved.

What should a driver do when travelling on a motorway or dual carriageway?
ABMW0484R

Be alert for other drivers who may suddenly change lanes or reduce speed.

Motorways and dual carriageways are designed to help traffic travel faster and more safely between destinations. Traffic conditions can change very quickly because of the speed and increased volumes of traffic and lanes, and you need to be particularly alert to other drivers changing lanes or reducing speed.

When driving on a motorway, what should a driver do?
ABMW0485R

Drive in the left-hand lane unless intending to overtake.

The normal 'keep left' rules apply when you are driving on a motorway – stay in the left lane unless you are overtaking.

When driving on a motorway, what should a driver do?
ABMW0486R

Be alert for other drivers who may suddenly change lane or reduce speed.

The normal 'keep left' rules apply when you are driving on a motorway – stay in the left lane unless you are overtaking.

Which statement is true about tyre pressure and driving on a motorway?

The driver should ensure that tyre pressure is normal.
ABMW0487R

You should ensure that the tyre pressure of your vehicle is correct at all times. Correct tyre pressure is especially important when travelling long distances, on motorways and at speed.

1
2
3

What should a driver do when joining a motorway from a slip road?

Try to match the vehicle speed to that of traffic already on the motorway and merge into it in a suitable gap.

ABMW0488R

When joining a motorway you should try to match your speed to that of the motorway traffic and merge into it when a suitable gap appears, while yielding to traffic already on the motorway.

Is a driver permitted to pick up or set down a passenger on a motorway?

No, this is not permitted.

ABMW0489R

Motorways are designed so that traffic can move faster and more freely. It is illegal and dangerous to stop a vehicle on any part of a motorway except in an emergency or when signalled to do so by a garda.

When driving on a motorway and wishing to turn back, what should a driver do?

ABMW0490R

Leave the motorway at the next exit and cross to the other side using the fly-over (or underpass).

If you miss your intended exit when driving on a motorway, you should proceed to the next junction exit where you can leave the motorway and then rejoin it in the opposite direction.

What should a driver do when leaving a motorway?

Comply with the speed limit on the road the driver is joining.

ABMW0492R

When you are leaving a motorway, enter the deceleration lane and reduce your speed. Comply with the speed limit of the road you are entering – most likely you will be in a 2-way traffic system where you will encounter vulnerable road users.

What should a driver do if they drive past their intended exit by mistake?
Drive on and leave at the next exit. ABMW0493R

If you miss your intended exit when driving on a motorway, you should proceed to the next
junction exit where you can leave the motorway and then rejoin it the opposite direction.

What is the difference between driving on a motorway and driving on other types of road?
ABMW0494R

Traffic usually travels at a higher speed on a motorway.

Motorways are designed so that traffic can move faster and more freely, without traffic
lights, crossroads, level crossings and other road features that might slow down traffic.
There are also restrictions on who may use a motorway – for example L-drivers and
motorcycles under 50cc are prohibited.

On a motorway, a driver wants to overtake another vehicle - what should the driver do?
ABMW0495R

Use their mirrors, signal and overtake in the right-hand lane.

When you want to overtake on a motorway, use the Mirror-Signal-Mirror (blind spots)-
Manoeuvre routine. Check your mirrors, signal your intention, check your mirrors again
(and your blind spots), and complete the manoeuvre when it is safe to do so. Pay particular
attention to the speed of the traffic behind you before you move out. When you have finished
overtaking, move back into the left-hand lane smoothly.

What may the hard shoulder of a motorway be used for?
Stopping in an emergency. ABMW0496R

There are extra dangers when driving on a motorway because of the increased volume of
traffic and higher speed. For safety reasons you must not drive or stop on the hard shoulder
of a motorway except in an emergency.

1
2
3

On exiting the motorway what should a driver do?

ABMW0497R

Be alert for oncoming and crossing traffic.

When leaving a motorway, enter the deceleration lane and reduce speed. Comply with the speed limits of the road you are entering. Be mindful that you are now driving in a 2-way traffic system where you will encounter vulnerable road users such as cyclists and pedestrians.

What should a driver do when leaving a motorway?

ABMW0498R

Obey the posted speed limit.

When leaving a motorway, enter the deceleration lane and reduce speed. Comply with the speed limits of the road you are entering. Be mindful that you are now driving in a 2-way traffic system where you will encounter vulnerable road users such as cyclists and pedestrians.

Junctions – roads of equal importance

A driver wishes to go straight ahead at a cross junction of equal importance - what should the driver do?

ABMW0499R

Give way to traffic approaching from the right.

At a cross junction of equal importance traffic approaching from the right has the right of way. It is important to understand that the right of way is not an absolute right. In such a situation, you should proceed with caution while showing due regard for other users of the road.

Clearways

What is a clearway?

ABMW0501R

An area where stopping and parking is not allowed during certain times.

You must not stop or park in a clearway area except outside the times stated on the information plate under the sign.

Parking on a hill

If you are parking on a hill, you should take steps to make sure that the vehicle does not roll down the hill after you have left it, and that there is no undue pressure on the handbrake.

What should a driver consider doing when parking a vehicle facing down a hill?
Angling the wheels towards the kerb.   ABMW0502R

When you are parking facing downhill, it is a good idea to angle the wheels towards the kerb. This will help to hold the vehicle in place and ease the pressure on the handbrake.

What should a driver considered doing when parking on a two-way street facing downhill?
Turning the steering wheel towards the kerb.   ABMW0503R

When you are parking on a two-way street facing downhill, it is a good idea to turn the steering wheel towards the kerb. This will assist the handbrake by easing the pressure needed to hold the vehicle. Where possible, park with the flow of traffic.

What should a driver consider doing when parking a vehicle on a two-way street and facing uphill?
Turning the steering wheel to the right.   ABMW0504R

If you are parking on a two-way street facing uphill, it is a good idea to turn the steering to the right. (away from the kerb) This means the kerb will help to hold the vehicle in place and reduce the pressure on the handbrake. Where possible, you should park with the flow of traffic.

1
2
3

Unmarked and narrow roads

You must know how to adopt the correct position when driving on an unmarked or narrow road. You need to be especially careful in these situations, as it may be difficult for you to see other road users and to be seen by them.

While driving on a primary road that is not divided by a central dividing line, what should a driver do?   ABMW0505R

Imagine there is a central line and drive on the left-hand side.

In the absence of road markings, you should take up a position far enough to the left to allow traffic to safely pass or overtake on the right but not so far to the left that you could endanger cyclists or pedestrians.

Roundabouts

The questions in this section check that you know how to negotiate roundabouts, and in particular that you know which lane to choose and understand that traffic already on the roundabout has right of way over someone about to enter it.

What should a driver do when approaching a roundabout?   ABMW0507R

Give way to traffic already on the roundabout.

You should always approach roundabouts with caution. Be prepared to give way to traffic already on the roundabout and to stop if necessary.

In what direction should a driver turn when entering a roundabout?

To the left. ABMW0508R

By law you must enter a roundabout by turning to the left and giving way to traffic already on the roundabout.

Where two lanes are provided on the approach to a roundabout, which lane should a driver select when they intend taking an exit to the right of the roundabout?

The right-hand lane. ABMW0509R

When you approach a roundabout where two lanes are provided, you should choose the most suitable one based on the exit you intend to take off the roundabout. The left lane is usually used for vehicles exiting to the left (9 o'clock) or straight ahead (12 o'clock) and the right is for vehicles exiting at any exit after 12 o'clock.

What position should a driver approach a roundabout when intending to take the first exit to the left?

ABMW0510R

Approach in the left-hand lane and give way to traffic already on the roundabout.

When you intend to take an exit to the left off a roundabout, you should always approach the roundabout in the left lane. Approach with caution and yield to traffic already on the roundabout.

What must a driver be aware of before entering a roundabout? ABMW0512R

The traffic to the right - how fast it's travelling and how close it is.

When you enter a roundabout, you must give way to traffic already on the roundabout approaching from your right. Do not enter a roundabout if by doing so you would force another vehicle to slow down or stop.

Turning right

Making a right-hand turn can be challenging, as it involves crossing the path of traffic coming in the opposite direction. The questions in this section check that you know how to make a right turn safely.

Where should a vehicle be positioned before turning right?
Just left of the centre of the road. ABMW0513R

The correct position to be in before turning right is just left of the centre of the road. Where the road is wide enough, this position allows traffic coming behind you and going straight ahead to pass you safely on the left.

What should a driver do before turning right from a major road into a minor road? ABMW0514R
Yield right of way to oncoming traffic and to pedestrians crossing at the junction.

You must yield to oncoming traffic when turning right from a major road to a minor road.

Driving in tunnels

If you are driving through a tunnel, your driving behaviour can present a hazard to yourself and to other road users. The questions in this section check that you understand how to drive in tunnels and how to respond to situations that might arise in a tunnel.

What should a driver do when entering a tunnel? ABMW0515R
Switch on dipped headlights.

Switch on your dipped headlights as you enter a tunnel.Switch on your dipped headlights as you enter a tunnel.

What should a driver do when entering a tunnel?
ABMW0516R

Keep a safe distance from the vehicle in front.

Tailgating could be particularly dangerous in a tunnel. The minimum recommended safe distance for a car or motorcycle is 50 metres and is 100 metres for all other vehicles.

What should a driver do when entering a tunnel?
ABMW0518R

Remove sunglasses and keep a safe distance from the vehicle in front.

As you enter the tunnel, turn on your dipped headlights and if you are wearing sunglasses, take them off. Pay attention for information signs displayed. While you are in the tunnel, keep a safe distance from the vehicle in front – the minimum safe distance for a car or motorcycle is 50 metres and for all other vehicles it's 100 metres.

When driving through a tunnel what should a driver do?
ABMW0519R

Keep further back than normal from the vehicle in front.

1

2

3

While you are driving in the tunnel, keep a safe distance from the vehicle in front – the minimum safe distance for a car or motorcycle is 50 metres and for all other vehicles it's 100 metres.

What should a driver do if there is traffic congestion in a tunnel?

Switch on hazard warning lights.
ABMW0520R

If there is traffic congestion in a tunnel, you should switch on hazard lights and remain patient. Keep a safe distance from the vehicle in front even in slow-moving traffic. Listen for traffic messages on the tunnel radio station, if available.

What should a driver do if traffic comes to a halt in a tunnel?

Switch off the engine.
ABMW0521R

If traffic comes to a halt in a tunnel, switch off your engine to prevent a build up of fumes in the tunnel. Stay patient and follow the instructions of the tunnel operators.

What should a driver do if their vehicle breaks down or they are involved in a collision in a tunnel? ABMW0522R

Switch on hazard warning lights and walk to emergency station to call for help.

If your vehicle breaks down or is involved in a collision in a tunnel, switch on your hazard warning lights, switch off your engine, go to an emergency station and use the emergency phone to alert the tunnel operator.

What should a driver do if their vehicle breaks down in a tunnel? ABMW0523R

Use the emergency telephone to call for help.

If your vehicle breaks down or is involved in a collision in a tunnel, switch on your hazard warning lights, switch off your engine, go to an emergency station and use the emergency phone to alert the tunnel operator.

What should a driver do in the event of a breakdown or incident in a tunnel? ABMW0524R

Switch on hazard lights and stop as close to the left-hand side as possible.

If your vehicle breaks down or is involved in a collision in a tunnel, switch on your hazard warning lights, switch off your engine, go to an emergency station and use the emergency phone to alert the tunnel operator.

What should a driver do if their vehicle goes on fire in a tunnel? ABMW0525R

Leave the vehicle and follow the emergency escape route.

If your vehicle goes on fire in a tunnel, you should stop the vehicle as soon as possible, evacuate any passengers to a safe place, go to an emergency station and use the emergency phone to alert the tunnel operator.

Vulnerable road users

While you are driving, most of the time you will be sharing the road with other road users, including some who are particularly vulnerable, such as pedestrians, cyclists and motorcyclists, and some who are inexperienced, unskilled or careless. You need to be particularly considerate of vulnerable road users.

1

2

3

Patience

When good drivers meet vulnerable road users, they show patience and courtesy. It never takes much extra time, and it is safer for all concerned.

When stopped at traffic lights and the green light comes on but pedestrians are still crossing the road, what should a driver do? ABMW0528R
Wait as long as necessary to enable them to complete the crossing.

A green traffic light means you should go if the way is clear. If pedestrians are crossing, give way to them and let them finish crossing before proceeding.

At traffic lights, a driver should take particular care for which road users coming up on the left? ABMW18
Motorcyclists.

Before moving off at traffic lights you should be aware of cyclists and motorcyclists coming up on the left – in particular where there is an advanced stop line for cyclists ahead of that for other road users.

What should a driver do when they see a slow moving vehicle up ahead being driven by a learner driver? ABMW0531R
Stay back until the driver can overtake safely.

You should be patient when driving behind a learner driver. Learners are not as experienced as other road users and may drive erratically.

What way is an inexperienced learner driver likely to react in traffic situations? ABMW0532R
Slower then an experienced driver.

You should be patient when driving behind a learner driver. Learners may not anticipate and react to situations as well as an experienced driver would.

1

2

3

At road junctions, what type of road users are particularly vulnerable?
Motorcyclists.   ABMW0535R

Vehicles do not have an automatic right of way at junctions. As a driver you should pay particular attention to vulnerable road users such as pedestrians, cyclists and motorcyclists and be aware that they are entitled to use the road in safety.

At traffic lights, a driver should take particular care for which road users coming up on the left?
Cyclists.   ABMW0536R

Before moving off at traffic lights you should be aware of cyclists and motorcyclists coming up on the left in general – in particular where there is an advanced stop line for cyclists ahead of that for other road users.

What should a driver do if the traffic light changes to green while pedestrians are still crossing at traffic lights or at a pelican crossing?
Wait patiently and let them cross at ease.   ABMW0537R

You must always yield to pedestrians already crossing at a pedestrian crossing or junction, and you must not hurry them off the crossing by aggressive actions. Vehicles do not have a greater right of way over other road users.

When a driver intends to make a left-hand turn on a busy city street junction and there are pedestrians and cyclists around, what should a driver do?
ABMW0538R

Watch for cyclists or pedestrians who may try to cross the road in front of your vehicle.

The vehicle does not have a greater right-of-way than any other road user. As a driver you should pay particular attention to vulnerable road users such as pedestrians, cyclists and motorcyclists and be aware that they are entitled to use the road in safety.

In slow-moving city traffic, a driver should occasionally check their blind spots for which road users in particular?
ABMW0539R

Cyclists.

In slow-moving city traffic, you should be aware of and check your blind spots before any manoeuvre. Cyclists can easily become 'hidden' in a blind spot, and in slow-moving traffic, they might be moving faster than you are.

1

2

3

At traffic lights a driver should take particular care for which road users coming up on the left?
ABMW0541R

Motorcyclists.

Before moving off at traffic lights you should be aware of cyclists and motorcyclists coming up on the left – in particular where there is an advanced stop line for cyclists ahead of that for other road users.

What should a driver do if while driving at 80km/h they see children on the road ahead?
ABMW0545R

Reduce speed and prepare to stop if necessary.

You should be aware that children can be unpredictable, and you should slow down and be prepared to stop if necessary.

At road junctions, what type of road users are particularly vulnerable?
Pedestrians.
ABMW16

Vehicles do not have an automatic right of way at junctions. As a driver you should pay particular attention to vulnerable road users such as pedestrians, cyclists and motorcyclists and be aware that they are entitled to use the road in safety.

When a driver intends to make a left-hand turn on a busy city street junction and there are pedestrians and cyclists around, what should a driver do?
ABMW19

Watch for cyclists or pedestrians on the left.

The vehicle does not have a greater right-of-way than any other road user. As a driver you should pay particular attention to vulnerable road users such as pedestrians, cyclists and motorcyclists and be aware that they are entitled to use the road in safety.

In slow-moving city traffic, a driver should occasionally check their blind spots for which road users in particular?
ABMW21

Motorcyclists.

In slow-moving city traffic, you should be aware of and check your blind spots before any manoeuvre. Motorcyclists can easily become 'hidden' in a blind spot, and in slow-moving traffic, they might be moving faster than you are.

In slow-moving city traffic a driver should occasionally check their blind spots for which road users in particular?
Pedestrians. ABMW22

In slow-moving city traffic, you should be aware of and check your blind spots before any manoeuvre. Pedestrians can easily become 'hidden' in a blind spot, and in slow-moving traffic, they might be moving faster than you are.

What should a driver do when driving at night on an unlit road?
Watch out for stray animals or livestock. ABMW24

While driving at night and even with the best headlights, it can be very difficult to see all the hazards that you might come across – for example, stray animals or livestock on the road. At night you should drive at a speed that will enable you to stop safely within the distance you can see to be clear ahead.

Clearance

While you are driving, you should make sure that you leave room (clearance) for other road users, particularly the more vulnerable ones, such as pedestrians (especially children and elderly people), cyclists and motorcyclists.

What should a driver do when overtaking a cyclist? ABMW0548R
Allow extra clearance in case the cyclist swerves suddenly.

You should never cut in front of cyclists when overtaking them. Give them plenty of space especially as they may change direction suddenly – for example, to avoid a pothole, or because they are blown off course by a strong gust of wind.

What should a driver do when they see joggers ahead on the left?
Check the mirrors, indicate and overtake the joggers, allowing them sufficient clearance. ABMW0549R

People on the road are more vulnerable than vehicles so you should treat them with care. If you see people jogging ahead, use the mirror–signal–mirror (blind spots)–manoeuvre routine and give sufficient clearance to the joggers when you are overtaking them.

When driving on a road that has a potholed surface and there is a cyclist ahead, what should a driver do? ABMW0550R
Allow extra clearance in case the cyclist swerves to avoid a pothole.

You should always be aware of how vulnerable cyclists are. When you are driving on a road with potholes or bad surfaces, take into account that they may have to swerve suddenly to avoid potholes.

1
2
3

Anticipation

It is sometimes hard to predict what another road user is going to do, and some categories of road user are particularly unpredictable. You should be prepared for pedestrians crossing the road unexpectedly, for children chasing a ball, for dogs or other animals running onto the roadway, for cyclists swerving to avoid a pothole, and for people in parked cars opening the door without warning. The questions in this section check that you understand the importance of anticipating such events and that you know how to take appropriate action.

What should a driver be aware of when making a left-hand turn? ABMW0552R
Cyclists might come up on the inside.

When you are turning left, you should be aware that cyclists and pedestrians may come up on your inside. Always check to your left before you make a left turn.

When driving through a residential area, what particular hazards should a driver be aware of? ABMW0554R
Children or residents may come out suddenly.

When driving through a built-up area, you should drive with care and always be ready for the unexpected – such as children running out onto the road.

When turning left into a side road, what should a driver do? ABMW0555R
Check for pedestrians or cyclists who may have come up on the 'inside'.

When you are turning left, you should be aware that cyclists and pedestrians may come up on your inside. Always check to your left before you make a left turn.

When driving on a country road without footpaths, what should a driver look out for coming towards them on their side of the road? ABMW0556R
Pedestrians.

Pedestrian deaths account for one in five fatalities on our roads, so you should always be on the look-out for pedestrians, especially on country roads where there is no footpath.

1

2

3

What should a driver do when driving at night on an unlit road? ABMW0557R
Watch out for pedestrians wearing dark clothing.

While driving at night and even with the best headlights, it can be very difficult to see all the hazards that you might come across – for example, pedestrians wearing dark clothing. At night you should drive at a speed that will enable you to stop safely within the distance you can see to be clear ahead.

What could happen if a driver parks on a footpath? ABMW0558R
Pedestrians could be impeded.

You should never park on a footpath. Pedestrians (including people with young children in pushchairs and prams) might have to go onto the road to get around your car, and this could put them in danger.

Signalling

If you drive in such a way that other road users have to brake suddenly or change their course dramatically, you can cause a collision. For that reason, it is important to give other road users adequate warning of your intention to slow down, stop, or change direction. Use your indicators.

What should a driver do when driving along and there is a cyclist on the road up ahead? ABMW0559R
Check the mirrors, indicate in good time and move out if it is safe to do so.

You should overtake only when it is safe to do so. Give extra space to cyclists when you are overtaking them, as they may need to move out to avoid a pothole, or they could be blown into your path on windy days.

If indicators are not fitted or are not working, how should signals be given? ABMW0560R
By hand, clearly and in good time.

If, for whatever reason, your vehicle does not have indicators or has indicators that are not working, you should know how to use the appropriate hand signals to alert other road users of your intention to change direction.

1
2
3

What should a driver do when travelling on a country road with following traffic, and they meet pedestrians?

ABMW0561R

Signal to following traffic their intention to overtake the pedestrians.

When you are driving on a road without footpaths, you should take extra care when you come upon pedestrians on the road. If you have to move out to overtake and there is following traffic, check your mirrors and signal in good time to alert the drivers behind that there is a hazard ahead.

Driving when the lighting is poor

At night, around dawn and dusk, and in bad weather, visibility can be significantly reduced. You need to keep a sharp look-out for other road users – particularly those that are more vulnerable, such as pedestrians and cyclists.

In relation to cyclists, what should a driver be aware of when driving on dark winter mornings and evenings on unlit country roads?

ABMW0562R

Cyclists are much more vulnerable in poor lighting conditions.

You should take extra care when driving on dark winter mornings and evenings – vulnerable road users such as cyclists and pedestrians (particularly schoolchildren) might not be so easy to see in low light conditions.

In relation to pedestrians, what should a driver be aware of when driving on dark winter mornings and evenings?

ABMW0564R

That there could be vulnerable pedestrians walking in the countryside.

You should take extra care when driving on dark winter mornings and evenings – vulnerable road users such as cyclists and pedestrians (particularly schoolchildren) might not be so easy to see in low light conditions.

In relation to pedestrians, what should a driver be aware of when driving on dark winter mornings and evenings?

ABMW0565R

Schoolchildren are more vulnerable on unlit country roads on dark winter mornings and evenings.

You should take extra care when driving on dark winter mornings and evenings – vulnerable road users such as cyclists and pedestrians (particularly schoolchildren) might not be so easy to see in low light conditions.

Necessary Documents

Before you drive any vehicle, you must hold a valid driving licence or learner permit for that category of vehicle, the vehicle must be properly taxed and insured, and you must be insured to drive it. You must carry your driving licence or learner permit with you while driving, and you must display up-to-date tax and insurance discs on the front windscreen of the vehicle.

Driving licences and learner permits

Your learner permit or driving licence imposes some restrictions on what you may and may not do when driving. The questions in this section check that you know the rules.

What drivers are required to display L-plates on their vehicle?

All Learner Permit holders except those driving agricultural tractors and works vehicles. ABMW0566R

All learner permit holders except those driving agricultural tractors or works vehicles are required to display L-plates on the front and rear of their vehicle. Learner permit holders in category A1, A and M are required to wear a yellow fluorescent tabard with an L- plate that is clearly visible on the front and back.

What restriction will be noted on a driver's full licence if they have passed their test on a vehicle with automatic transmission? ABMW0567R

They may not drive vehicles with manual transmission.

If you pass your driving test in a vehicle fitted with automatic transmission, a code 78 will be noted on the full licence in the restrictions / information column.

What roads are learner permit holders allowed to drive on? ABMW0568R

All roads except motorways.

A learner permit holder must not drive on a motorway. It is a serious offence to do so.

How should an L-plate be composed? ABMW0569R

A red L on a white background.

L-plates should be displayed front and rear. The plates should be a red L on a white background and should be not less than 15cm high with a border of at least 2cm. A learner motorcyclist must wear a yellow tabard displaying L-plates front and rear. The L-plates must be not less than 15cm high on a white background.

Which roads are Learner Permit holders not allowed to drive on?

They may not drive on motorways. ABMW0570R

A learner permit holder must not drive on a motorway. It is a serious offence to do so.

Which learner permit holders are exempt from having to be accompanied by qualified drivers?

Learner permit holders in categories A, A1 and M.

Learner permit holders in categories A, A1 and M do not have to be accompanied by qualified drivers. Learner permit holders in these categories must not carry a passenger.

Where can drivers locate the Gross Vehicle Weight of their vehicle?

On a metal plate on the vehicle. ABMW0781R

The plate displaying the Gross Vehicle Weight of a vehicle is normally located under the bonnet or in the passenger compartment. If you are not sure where it is located on your vehicle, check the driver's handbook supplied with the vehicle.

1
2
3

Vehicle registration and motor tax

Vehicles are registered when they are first sold or imported. The registration details are recorded in the vehicle registration document or vehicle licensing certificate – these details include the engine number and the vehicle registration number (which is shown on the registration plate at the front and back of the vehicle).

Vehicles that are used on public roads must be taxed at all times, and they must display a current tax disc at all times.

Is it permitted to use a vehicle in a public place without a current tax disc displayed?

ABMW0586R

No, all motor vehicles must be taxed before the vehicle is taken on the road.

A motor vehicle must be taxed and must display the up-to-date tax disk before it may be taken on the road.

If a driver wishes to drive a vehicle but the tax disc is expired, what should they do?

ABMW0588R

They should not drive it.

A motor vehicle must be taxed and must display the up-to-date tax disc before it may be taken on the road.

If a driver wishes to drive another vehicle which is not currently taxed, would they be allowed to transfer the current tax disc from their own vehicle onto it?

ABMW0589R

No, tax discs are not transferable.

A motor vehicle must be taxed and must display its own up-to-date tax disc before it may be taken on the road. The tax disc includes information about the vehicle, including its make and model, colour and registration number.

When a vehicle is being driven by a person who is not its owner, who should ensure that the correct tax disc is displayed?

The driver and the owner of the vehicle are equally responsible.

ABMW0590R

If you are the owner or the driver of a vehicle, you must ensure that it is taxed and that it displays an up-to-date tax disc before you take it on the road.

When must a current tax disc be displayed on a new vehicle on a public road?

ABMW0591R

At all times.

A motor vehicle must be taxed before it may be taken on the road, and it must always display an up-to-date tax disc.

Who may demand to see a driver's vehicle registration document / vehicle licensing certificate?

ABMW0592R

Any garda.

A garda may demand to see your driving licence at any time, and you should always carry this with you when driving. A garda may also examine your insurance disc, tax disc and NCT disc (if applicable). A garda may ask you to produce other documents (including the vehicle's registration document) at a named garda station within 10 days.

Insurance

Before you drive any vehicle, you must make sure that the vehicle is insured and that you are insured to drive it. It is a serious offence to drive without proper insurance. The questions in this section check that you fully understand this issue.

When a vehicle is being driven by a person who is not its owner but who has the owner's consent, who should ensure that the vehicle is properly insured?

ABMW0593R

Both the driver and the vehicle owner.

All drivers must have insurance covering them to drive a vehicle on a public road. It is a serious offence to drive a vehicle that is not insured. It is also an offence to allow a vehicle that you own to be driven by an uninsured driver.

Is a driver still insured to drive their vehicle after their insurance policy has expired?

ABMW0594R

No, the vehicle is not insured after the expiry of the policy.

All drivers must have insurance covering them to drive a vehicle on a public road. The vehicle must display an up-to-date insurance disc. Insurance companies insist that the premium must be paid before the renewal date.

If a driver wishes to drive another privately-owned vehicle but they are uncertain if they are insured to drive, what should they do?

ABMW0595R

A driver should contact their own insurer to confirm whether or not their insurance policy covers the driving of other vehicles.

If you are in any doubt about your insurance cover, you should discuss the matter with your insurance company. It is a serious offence to drive a vehicle that is not insured.

When a driver wishes to drive a vehicle and they are not sure if they are covered by insurance, what should they do?

ABMW0596R

They should not drive until cover is confirmed by their insurance company.

If you are in any doubt about your insurance cover, you should discuss the matter with your insurance company. It is a serious offence to drive a vehicle that is not insured.

1
2
3

What is the minimum insurance cover which is required to drive a vehicle on a public road?
ABMW0597

Third Party.

As a motorist must have a minimum of third party insurance. This indemnifies you against any claim made against you.

What information must a driver give in order to obtain insurance cover on a vehicle?
ABMW0598R

All information requested by the insurance company.

All drivers must have insurance covering them to drive a vehicle on a public road. The law imposes a duty on drivers to give their insurance company any relevant information before driving a vehicle.

If the owner of a vehicle has had the engine capacity of the vehicle altered, what should they do?
ABMW0599R

Inform their local motor taxation office and their insurance company.

The law imposes a duty on drivers to give their insurance company any relevant information before driving a vehicle. This includes details of any modifications made to the vehicle. In the case of a change of engine capacity, you must inform the local Motor Taxation Office, as different rates of motor tax may apply.

If a driver passes their test using a vehicle with automatic transmission, which vehicles are they licensed to drive?
ABMW0601R

Automatic vehicles only.

If you pass your driving test in an automatic or adapted vehicle, your full licence will apply to that type of vehicle only. A licence restricted to automatic vehicles will have a code 78 indicated in the restrictions / information column of the licence.

Collisions

At the scene of a collision, whether or not you were
involved in it, your first concern should be to make sure
that any injured persons are properly attended to by
contacting the emergency services. Your second concern
should be to make sure that the situation does not get any
worse – this means making sure that oncoming traffic is
given adequate warning of the hazard and that bystanders
are not exposed to danger.

If the vehicle you are driving is involved in a collision, you
must exchange information with the other driver, and
you should report the incident to the Gardaí and to your
insurance company.

1

2

3

Taking action

If you are involved in a collision, or if you arrive at the scene of a collision, you can help by calling the emergency services and by making sure that the situation does not get any worse. Do not take any action that might endanger yourself or anyone else, and administer first-aid only if you have been trained to do so.

How can a driver assist a motorcyclist who is in shock on the road following an incident?
ABMW0602R

Lie the motorcyclist on their side in the recovery position.

If you arrive at the scene of a collision, always call the emergency services on 999 or 112. Only properly trained persons should assist victims at the scene of an incident. If a victim is conscious, you may help put them in the recovery position until the emergency services arrive. Never move a collision victim unless there is a danger of fire or of a vehicle turning over.

What should a driver do when involved in an incident where nobody is injured but the vehicles are causing a danger or obstruction on the road?
Mark the position of the vehicles and move them off the road. ABMW0611R

In a collision where nobody is injured and there is only minor damage to vehicles, the vehicles should be moved to the side of the road to ensure that they do not cause an obstruction or endanger other road users.

What should a driver do if involved in an incident where they feel it was the fault of another driver?
ABMW0612R

Stop immediately and exchange particulars with the other person involved.

If you are involved in any sort of incident with another motorist, you should always exchange insurance details with the other driver and take note of the other vehicle's make and model, colour and registration number. Report the incident to the Gardaí. In a collision where nobody is injured and there is only minor damage to vehicles, the vehicles should be moved to the side of the road to ensure that they do not cause an obstruction or endanger other road users.

If a driver is involved in a collision, when should they inform their insurance company?
ABMW0613R

As soon as they possibly can.

If you are involved in an incident with another vehicle, you should inform your insurance company as soon as possible. This will help with any claims that may be made by another party against your insurance company.

Collision – no injury

If you are involved in a collision in which nobody is injured and the damage to property is minor, you do not have to involve the Gardaí. You should, however, exchange your contact details and insurance information with the other driver, and make a note of when, where and how the collision happened, in case the incident becomes the subject of an insurance claim later.

What should a driver do if involved in an incident where there is damage to property only? ABMW0615R

It is not necessary to report it to the Gardai provided it has been reported to the property owner.

If you are involved in an incident where the only damage is to property (for example, a garden wall or fence or a parked car), you must report it to the owner or to the person in charge of the property, or to the Gardaí if nearby. If you cannot do his, you should report the incident to a Garda station as soon as possible.

1

2

3

Collision – person injured

If you are involved in a collision and somebody is injured you must immediately contact the emergency services by dialling 112 or 999. You must stay at the scene of the collision and make a report to the Gardaí. You should if possible exchange your contact details and insurance information with the other driver. It is advisable to make a note of when, where and how the collision happened, so that you can provide these details to your insurance company.

What should a driver do where a person has been injured in a collision?

Move the victim only if there is a risk of fire or further injury. ABMW0616R

Never move an injured person at the scene of a collision unless there is a risk of fire or further injury. Moving an injured person could add to their injuries. Trained personnel know best how to attend to injured persons. Call the emergency services (on 999 or 112) or make sure that someone else has called them.

What type of drink should be given to a person who has been injured in a collision?
ABMW0617R

No drink should be given.

A person who has been injured in a collision should not be given anything to drink, as this could cause them to choke. Only trained personnel should attend to an injured person. Call the emergency services (on 999 or 112) or make sure that someone else has called them.

What should a driver do to assist a person who is unconscious following a collision?
ABMW0618R

Loosen tight clothing around the neck and keep the person warm with a blanket or overcoat.

If a person is unconscious following a collision, you should loosen tight clothing around the their neck and keep them warm with a blanket or overcoat until the emergency services arrive. Call the emergency services (on 999 or 112) or make sure that someone else has called them.

What should a driver do if they arrive at the scene of a collision and a person is bleeding heavily?
ABMW0619R

Try to stop the bleeding by putting on a tight bandage.

If you arrive at the scene of a collision and someone is bleeding heavily, you can try to stop the flow of blood by putting on a tight bandage. Call the emergency services (on 999 or 112) or make sure that someone else has called them.

Who should first be contacted where a person has been injured in a collision?
ABMW0621R

The emergency services.

Where somebody has been injured in a collision, it is important to call the emergency services immediately on 999 or 112. Trained emergency services personnel know best how to attend to injured persons.

Exchange of information

If you are involved in a collision with another vehicle, you should ask the driver of the other vehicle for their contact details (name, address, telephone number) and the details of their insurance cover (insurance company and policy number). You should also note the registration number, make and model of their vehicle. At the same time, you should provide the other driver with your own details and those of your vehicle. You will need all these details to report the incident to the Gardaí or to your insurance company.

If a driver is involved in a collision with an uninsured visiting motorist, where nobody is injured, who should it be reported to?   ABMW0623R
The driver's insurance company and the Gardai.

If you are involved in any type of collision, you should always report it to the Gardai and to your insurance company.

What should a driver do if involved in a collision with another vehicle where nobody is injured?   ABMW0624R
Exchange all relevant details with the other driver and report it to the Gardai.

If a you are involved in a collision with another vehicle where nobody is injured, you should exchange all the relevant details with the other driver – including name, address, vehicle registration, make and model and all insurance details.

Hazardous materials

If you are involved in a collision with a vehicle carrying hazardous materials, or if you arrive at the scene of such a collision, you should take steps to make sure that the situation does not deteriorate. Do not take any action that might endanger yourself or others. Call the emergency services and try to warn other road users of the danger.

What should a driver do if they arrive at the scene of a collision involving a vehicle carrying hazardous materials?   ABMW0625R
Keep well clear and raise the alarm.

If you arrive at the scene of a collision involving a vehicle carrying hazardous materials, you should keep well clear of the scene. Call the emergency services on 999 or 112 and give them as much information as you can about the marking labels on the vehicle. You should also warn other road users about the danger.

1
2
3

Safety considerations relating to loads and passengers

The questions in this section are designed to check that you understand the effects of severe braking on the people and goods in your vehicle, and that you know the importance of keeping the loads you carry in the vehicle within the limits set by the manufacturer.

Severe braking

By planning your journey, reading the road ahead, developing an awareness of the traffic conditions around you, and driving at an appropriate speed, you can generally avoid the need for sudden or harsh braking. On the occasions when you do have to apply the brakes severely, you need to be aware of the effects on yourself, your passengers and any goods in the vehicle.

What danger can arise if a driver has to brake suddenly? ABMW0626R
Both the driver and passengers could be thrown forward.

When you brake suddenly, the balance of weight of the vehicle is shifted forward, and this may cause the occupants and any loose objects in the vehicle to be thrown forward.

What should a driver do to avoid the need for harsh braking? ABMW0627R
Look ahead and anticipate what others may do.

You should know what speed you're travelling at and you should always drive at a speed that is appropriate to the conditions you are driving in, and you should be able to stop smoothly and safely within the distance you can see to be clear ahead.

Vehicle carrying capacity and load distribution

Every vehicle is certified by its manufacturer to have a maximum safe load-carrying capacity, and a maximum towing capacity. You must not exceed these limits: it is illegal to do so, and can be extremely dangerous. The questions in this section check that you understand this important issue.

How does the driver know a vehicle's total load-carrying capacity?
By referring to the vehicle manufacturer's specification. ABMW0628R

Design Gross Vehicle Weight is the term used by manufacturers for the weight of the vehicle together with the maximum load it is designed to carry. Drivers must understand the carrying capacity of their vehicle. Overloading your vehicle will make it more difficult to control, and it's an offence.

What determines the maximum allowed towing capacity of a vehicle?
The manufacturer's specifications. ABMW0629

The maximum weight that your vehicle can safely tow is specified by the manufacturer, and is usually set out in the driver's handbook for the vehicle, and in some cases on a plate attached to the vehicle. This is the safe towing limit for the vehicle and you should not exceed it.

What effect does overloading a vehicle have on its road-holding?
The load can make the vehicle more difficult to control. ABMW0630

Overloading your vehicle will make it more difficult to control. Remember: it's an offence to overload a vehicle.

What would be the effect of overloading a vehicle with passengers or goods?
ABMW0631R

It would reduce the driver's ability to control the vehicle.

Overloading your vehicle will make it more difficult to control, and will increase the risk of a collision

What effect could an unevenly distributed load have on a vehicle?
ABMW0632R

It could make the vehicle unstable while turning a corner or braking.

When loading a vehicle you should ensure that the load is distributed evenly. An unevenly distributed load may change the vehicle's centre of gravity and this could affect the braking and steering.

Technical matters with a bearing on road safety

The questions in this section check that you know how to keep your vehicle in good condition, that you recognise signs that it needs to be repaired or serviced, and that you understand the implications for your own safety and that of others of a vehicle in poor condition.

Headlights

When you are driving at night or in poor visibility, the headlights on your vehicle are essential for two reasons: they enable you to see the road ahead, and they enable other drivers and road users to see your vehicle. For these reasons, the headlights on the vehicle must be working properly at all times.

Why is it important to ensure that the vehicle headlights are correctly aligned?
ABMW0633R

To enable the driver to see properly.

You should ensure that your headlights are properly aligned and clean. When dipped, properly aligned headlights are less likely to dazzle oncoming traffic .

What effect could incorrectly aligned headlights have?
ABMW0635R

They could dazzle oncoming drivers.

A driver should ensure their headlights are properly aligned so as not to dazzle oncoming drivers and also to see properly themselves.

In general, how frequently should a vehicle's lights be checked?
ABMW0636R

Regularly.

You are responsible for your vehicle's roadworthiness and you should check it at regular intervals. Among the checks you should make are that all the lights are in working order.

1
2
3

What effect can a broken lens have on a headlight?
ABMW0637R

It can reduce and distort the beam.

You are responsible for your vehicle's roadworthiness and you should check it at regular intervals. Among the checks you should make are that all the lights are in working order. If you find defects in the lights, you should have them repaired as soon as possible.

A driver wishes to drive at night, but their right-hand headlight bulb is blown. What should the driver do?
ABMW0638R

Not drive until the bulb is replaced.

You must not drive on the road unless your vehicle's headlights are in good working order and adjusted properly.

Which of the following is a driver required to keep in good condition?
Headlights.
ABMW0639R

1
2
3

You are responsible for your vehicle's roadworthiness and you should check it at regular intervals. Among the checks you should make are that all the lights, (including the headlights) are in working order.

Brake lights

The brake lights on your vehicle provide a visible warning to traffic coming behind you that you are slowing and may be stopping. They must be kept in working order.

How would a driver know if a brake-light bulb was not working?
ABMW0640R

By standing at the rear of the vehicle and checking as another person presses the brake pedal.

To help you to be sure that the rear brake lights are working correctly, ask someone to stand outside the car and to check that the lights come on when you press the brake pedal.

Is it permissible to drive a vehicle on a public road when the brake lights are not working?
ABMW0642R

No, it is never permitted to be driven.

You must ensure that your vehicle's brake-lights are clean and working correctly before driving on a public road.

Dashboard lights

Modern engines are equipped with sophisticated systems for monitoring the condition of the engine and other parts of the vehicle, and for warning the driver if something goes wrong. These warnings are generally in the form of a warning light on the dashboard.

What does this light mean?
ABMW0643R
The battery is not charging.

If the battery warning light comes on, it means there is some kind of problem with the electrical charging system of the vehicle and the battery isn't being charged properly.

What does this light mean?
ABMW0644R
The high-beam headlights are switched on.

All vehicles are fitted with warning lights to alert you to different things. This light comes on when your full beam headlights are turned on.

What does this light mean?
ABMW0645
Low oil level.

If the oil pressure warning light comes on, it means that the oil pressure has dropped. You should not drive the vehicle until the problem is fixed.

What does this light mean?
ABMW0646R
Directional indicator on.

All vehicles are fitted with warning lights to alert you to different things. This light tells you that the directional indicator is on.

What should a driver do if a warning light starts flashing on the dashboard of their vehicle?
ABMW0650R
Stop and check the problem.

If a warning light starts flashing while you are driving, you should stop in a safe place and investigate the problem before deciding what action to take.

What should a driver do if a red warning light lights up on the dashboard of their vehicle?

ABMW0651R

Stop and investigate the cause.

If a warning light comes on while you are driving, you should stop in a safe place and investigate the problem before deciding what action to take.

Reflectors

What is the purpose of the vehicle's reflectors?

ABMW0652R

They reflect light at night to make other road users aware of the vehicle.

Motor vehicles are fitted with reflectors to make it easier to be seen by other road users. Keep your reflectors clean to ensure they are most effective.

Indicators

When a driver operates the indicator switch and hears a more rapid clicking noise than normal, what could this mean?

ABMW0653R

An indicator bulb has blown.

A rapid clicking noise when you turn on an indicator is usually a sign that one of the indicator bulbs has failed. You are responsible for making sure that your vehicle is roadworthy. This should include a regular check that all your lights, including indicators, are working properly.

Brakes

What does ABS do?

ABMW0654

It prevents the wheels from locking under harsh braking conditions.

Anti-lock braking system (ABS) is a type of braking system found in most modern cars. It comes into play automatically when you brake harshly. In the wet it can help prevent the wheels from skidding so that you can continue to steer while braking. ABS does not reduce the braking distance.

1
2
3

If the brake pedal of a vehicle feels soft or spongy when applied, what does this mean?

ABMW0655R

A fault in the brake fluid system.

If the brake pedal feels soft or spongy when you press it, it could indicate that the brake fluid level is low and there is a fault in the system. Each time you set out on a journey, test your brakes. Check the brake fluid level regularly.

How would a driver know if the brake fluid in their vehicle is low?

The brakes feel spongy and soft.

ABMW0656R

If the brake pedal feels soft or spongy when you press it, it could indicate that the brake fluid level is low and there is a fault in the system. Check the brake fluid level regularly, and test the brakes each time you set out on a journey.

What is a possible consequence of driving a vehicle in which the brake fluid level is low?

ABMW0657R

The vehicle could fail to stop when the brakes are applied, leading to a collision.

For your brakes to work correctly, you need to make sure that the brake fluid is kept at the correct level. If the brake fluid is low, the brakes will feel spongy or soft, they won't work as well as they should and this will increase your stopping distance. Low brake fluid could be the difference between stopping safely and having a collision.

If a driver applies the foot brake and hears a scraping noise, what is the most likely cause?

ABMW0658R

The brake linings or pads are worn.

You should test your brakes before setting out on a journey. If when driving you a scraping noise when you press the brake, the most likely reason is that the brake linings or pads are worn. In this case, your brakes won't work as well as they should. Have worn brake linings or pads replaced immediately.

How does a driver know when there is a problem with the brakes in their vehicle?

ABMW0659R

The vehicle's stopping ability is affected.

You should test your brakes before setting out on a journey. If when you are braking you notice that it takes longer than usual to bring the vehicle to a stop, you should have the brakes checked by a mechanic immediately.

After changing a wheel on a vehicle, which of the following should be checked soon afterwards?

ABMW26

The tyre pressure.

After you have changed a wheel on a vehicle, you should check the tyre pressure on the replacement wheel to make sure it is correct.

Automatic transmission

A vehicle with automatic transmission has some obvious differences from one with manual transmission (such as no clutch), and some differences that are not so obvious. You need to be aware of these differences, particularly if you sometimes drive a manual vehicle and sometimes an automatic.

If driving a vehicle with automatic transmission, what in particular should a driver be aware of?

ABMW0660R

That engine braking power is reduced.

When you are driving an automatic vehicle and you release the acceleratior, the vehicle will not slow at the same rate as a vehicle with a manual gearbox. You should be aware of this, as you may need to apply the brake earlier in order to stop where required.

What effect does automatic transmission have on engine braking power?

It reduces it.

ABMW0661

When driving an automatic vehicle and you release the acceleration, the vehicle will not slow at the same rate as a vehicle with a manual gearbox. You should be aware of this, as you may need to apply the brake earlier in order to stop where required.

Vehicle condition (engine)

For your comfort and safety, and those of your passengers and other road users, you should make sure that the engine in your vehicle is operating properly. Have it serviced regularly, in line with the manufacturer's recommendations.

What does this dial provide information on?
Engine revolution.   ABMW0662R

The rev counter measures the speed of the engine. in 'revolutions per minute' Generally, the higher the revs, the more fuel the engine is using, so you should keep an eye on the rev counter to help you drive in a more eco-friendly manner.

What does a rev counter provide information on?
Engine revolutions.   ABMW0663R

The rev counter measures the speed of the engine. in 'revolutions per minute' Generally, the higher the revs, the more fuel the engine is using, so you should keep an eye on the rev counter to help you drive in a more eco-friendly manner.

If, when driving along, the driver notices that the engine power is lower than normal, what should they do?
Have the vehicle checked by a competent mechanic.   ABMW0664R

If when driving you notice that the vehicle seems underpowered, you should have the it checked by a competent mechanic as soon as possible. This could be a symptom of one of a number of problems.

Which of the following is a driver required to keep in good condition?
Seatbelts.   ABMW25

You are responsible for your vehicle's roadworthiness and you should check it at regular intervals. Among the checks you should make are that all the seatbelts (driver's and passengers') are in good working order.

Oil and fuel

The oil in your engine lubricates and cools the moving parts of the engine. If there is too little oil in the engine, or if it is not reaching the parts that need it, the engine can be permanently damaged.

You should, of course, make sure that you have sufficient fuel (petrol or diesel, depending on the type of engine) in the tank to take you safely to your destination.

What is the purpose of engine oil? ABMW0670R
It lubricates the engine components.

The purpose of engine oil is to lubricate and cool the moving parts of the engine.

If the oil gauge shows little or no pressure, what could the problem be?
The oil level is too low. ABMW0665R

You should check the oil level in your vehicle regularly, and if it is low, top it up. If you find you have to top up very often, you should have the vehicle checked by a mechanic to see if there is a problem.

What may happen if the vehicle's engine oil is not changed regularly?
Parts of the engine may suffer increased wear. ABMW0666R

Engine oil becomes dirty over time and must be changed. The oil change is usually done when the vehicle is being serviced.

If a vehicle is driven with low oil pressure, what effect does this have on its engine? ABMW0667R
It increases wear and tear on the engine.

Low oil pressure is usually related to low oil level or to a faulty oil pump. You should check the oil level in your vehicle regularly, and if it is low, top it up. If you find you have to top up very often, you should have the vehicle checked by a mechanic to see if there is a problem.

1
2
3

If the vehicle's oil-pressure gauge is reading low or the red oil-pressure warning light comes on, what should a driver do? ABMW0668R

Drive to a safe place, stop the vehicle and check the oil level.

Oil circulation is essential for the safe running of your vehicle's engine. If the warning lights or gauges tell you that the oil is low or the pressure is low, you should stop as soon as you can in safe place, check the oil level, and top up if necessary. Continuing to drive may damage the engine. If the problem is not just related to the oil level, you should have the vehicle checked by a mechanic.

What should someone do before checking the engine oil level on a vehicle? ABMW0669R

Make sure that the engine is switched off.

You should have a basic knowledge of the regular checks that should be carried out on your vehicle. Checking the engine oil level is important – do this with the engine switched off.

What is the function of an engine oil filter? ABMW0671R

It prevents the circulation of sediment in the oil.

The oil filter collects impurities and sediment from the oil and so helps to reduce damage and wear and tear on the engine. The oil filter must be changed regularly – this is usually done when the vehicle is being serviced.

While driving, a driver notices a strong smell of fuel. What should they do? ABMW0672R

Stop where safe and investigate.

A strong smell of fuel is usually an indication that something is wrong, and you should stop and investigate as soon as possible. Leaking or spilling petrol can be dangerous because it is so combustible, and leaking diesel fuel can make the road very slippery.

What does the warning light and /or red zone on a fuel gauge mean?

The level of fuel in the tank is low. ABMW0674R

Many vehicles are fitted with various warning lights and gauges. A red zone or a warning light on a fuel gauge means the vehicle is low in fuel and should be re-fueled as soon as possible.

Coolant temperature

While it is running, the engine in your vehicle heats up, but if it overheats, it may be permanently damaged. To prevent this, the main parts of the engine are kept at the correct temperature by the circulation of cooling fluid. You must make sure that there is sufficient coolant in the reservoir, and that you do not drive if the temperature gauge or warning light indicates that the engine is overheating.

When is it recommended to use coolant or antifreeze?
All year round.

ABMW0673R

The purpose of coolant is to keep the engine cool during operation. Coolant is usually a mixture of water and anti-freeze – this ensures that the coolant does not freeze in very cold weather.

While driving, the driver notices the vehicle temperature gauge showing red. What should they do?
Stop in a safe place and have the problem investigated.

ABMW0677R

Many vehicles are fitted with various warning lights and gauges. A warning light or a red zone on a temperature gauge means the engine is starting to overheat and the vehicle should not be driven until the problem is rectified.

What should a driver do if they notice steam rising from the engine compartment?
Stop where safe and investigate the cause.

ABMW0678R

When a vehicle shows signs of overheating, you should stop in a safe place and investigate the problem. Do not drive a vehicle whose engine is overheating, as this could damage the engine.

When is it recommended to use coolant?
All year round.

ABMW0679R

The purpose of coolant is to keep the engine cool during operation. Coolant is usually a mixture of water and anti-freeze – this ensures that the coolant does not freeze in very cold weather.

Body condition

If the body of your vehicle is damaged or rusted, it can be more dangerous. For example, if there are sharp or jagged edges, these can cause serious injury if the vehicle is involved in a collision – even a minor one. You should also ensure that the shock absorbers are functioning correctly, or the vehicle may become unstable and difficult to control.

If a driver notices that parts of their vehicle's body have been affected by rust, what should they do?   ABMW0680R
Have it repaired by a competent repair shop.

Over time vehicles may become affected by rust to various degrees. You should inspect your vehicle's body periodically and if you find signs of rust you should have it assessed and repaired if necessary to prevent further deterioration.

What effect can a worn shock absorber have on a vehicle?   ABMW0682R
It can cause the vehicle to 'bounce' in an unstable manner.

A worn shock absorber can make a vehicle difficulty to control especially on uneven surfaces and it can increase stopping distance.

Battery

In a petrol- or diesel-powered vehicle, the engine is started by a small electric motor, which is powered by a 12-volt battery. This battery also supplies power to the lights and other electrical appliances, but only when the engine is not running. When the engine is running, it drives an alternator to produce electricity, and this both recharges the battery and supplies power to the lights and other electrical appliances.

What happens if the vehicle has a flat battery?   ABMW0675R
The engine will not start.

All motor vehicles have a battery to supply power, primarily to start the engine. If the battery is flat, you will not be able to start the engine in the normal way. When the engine is running, it produces its own electricity to recharge the battery and run the various electrical components, including lights, heating, the radio and so on.

What is the purpose of the battery fitted to a petrol- or diesel-powered motor vehicle?

ABMW0676R

To start the engine.

The primary purpose of the battery is to start the engine. When the engine is running, it produces its own electricity to charge the battery and run the various electrical components, including lights, heating, radio and so on.

What effect would a weakly charged battery have on a vehicle's driving performance?

ABMW0681R

It would have no effect.

It might be difficult to start a car with a weak battery, but once the engine is running, it makes no difference. You should replace the battery before it runs out completely.

Mirrors

The exterior mirrors on each side of the vehicle and the interior rear-view mirror are important pieces of safety equipment. While you are driving, they enable you to see behind and to the side of your vehicle without turning your head, so that you can maintain your view of the road ahead. Before starting a journey, you should make sure that they are in good condition and properly adjusted.

What should the driver be able to see in the vehicle mirrors when they have been properly adjusted?

ABMW0683R

The area behind and to each side of the vehicle.

Your mirrors enable you to see the road behind and to the sides. This helps you to take into account what's happening behind you, so that you can make informed, correct and safe decisions.

What should the driver be able to see in the exterior mirrors of a vehicle when they have been properly adjusted?

ABMW0684R

The sides of the vehicle and the roads to the side

Exterior mirrors enable you to see to the side of the vehicle, and to take into account all visible hazards and make correct and safe decisions.

The vehicle's exterior mirrors are covered by a film of mud and dust. What should the driver do? ABMW0685
Clean them with a cloth or tissue before continuing on.

The purpose of mirrors is to increase the drivers view to enable them to take into account all visible hazards and make correct and safe decisions. A driver should ensure that the wing mirrors are clean and properly adjusted at all times otherwise their view will be hindered.

When a driver is making a left-hand turn, what mirrors should they particularly concentrate on? ABMW0686R
The interior and left exterior mirror.

When you are turning left, you should be aware that cyclists and other vehicles may come up on your inside. For that reason it is particularly important to check your left exterior mirror and your internal mirror before turning. Always use the mirror–signal–mirror (blind spots)–manouevre routine when you are turning and be extra careful If you have to cross a bus lane to make the turn.

What effect can wet weather have on a vehicle's exterior mirrors?
Water droplets can obscure the reflected image. ABMW0687

In rain and damp conditions, small water droplets can form on the glass of the exterior mirrors. This could make it more difficult to see the road behind and to the sides. Switch on the mirror demisters, if you have them.

Exhaust

The exhaust system on a vehicle takes away the gases and other by-products of the engine's combustion process. In doing so, it filters them to make them less damaging to the environment, and it reduces the noise created by the engine. It is important to make sure that the exhaust system is in good condition – if it is not working correctly, poisonous fumes may enter the vehicle, with lethal consequences.

What does blue smoke coming from the vehicle's exhaust mean?
The engine is burning oil. ABMW0688R

As an engine gets old or if it is not properly maintained, it can 'burn oil' and give off 'blue smoke' from the exhaust. This is harmful to the atmosphere and should be corrected.

What is the effect of a worn exhaust? ABMW0689R
The filtering of fumes is reduced and engine noise is louder.

A worn exhaust system can have a number of effects, including increased noise from the engine and more fumes (as as they are not filtered properly).

How can a faulty exhaust affect your vehicle? ABMW0690R
It can increase the noise and pollution levels.

A worn exhaust system can have a number of effects, including increased noise from the engine and more fumes (as they are not filtered properly).

What is the purpose of a catalytic converter? ABMW0691R
It filters exhaust gases and reduces air pollution.

The purpose of a catalytic converter (CAT) is to remove toxic or polluting gases such as carbon monoxide, nitrogen oxide and unburned hydrocarbons from the exhaust emissions.

1
2
3

Tyres and wheels

Your ability to control your vehicle, to steer it in the direction you want and to stop it when and where you want depends critically on the few square centimetres of rubber that are in contact with the road at any time. You must make sure that your tyres are in good condition and correctly inflated. The questions in this section check that you know how to do this.

What does the speed rating of a tyre indicate?

The maximum speed for which the tyre is designed.   ABMW0692R

The speed rating of a tyre is the maximum speed for which the tyre is designed. This relates to the speed capability of the tyre. It does not relate to the speed at which the tyre should or could legally be driven.

Why should the valve be replaced when having a tubeless tyre fitted?

To ensure the tyre will stay inflated.   ABMW0693R

When fitting a new tubeless tyre to a vehicle it is a good idea to change the valve also, because it has presumably been on the wheel since the old tyre was fitted; and it could break down, leak and cause the air to escape.

After changing a wheel on a vehicle, which of the following should be checked soon afterwards?

ABMW0694R

The wheel nuts.

After you have changed a wheel on a vehicle it is a good idea to check the wheel nuts after a short period of driving to ensure they are still properly secured.

In general, how often should a driver check the tyre pressure of a vehicle?

ABMW0696R

Regularly.

As a driver, it is your legal responsibility to make sure that your vehicle is roadworthy. To do this, you should carry out weekly and periodical checks, including a weekly tyre pressure check.

Why should tyres be kept at the pressure specified by the manufacturer?
To help provide optimum roadholding. ABMW0697R

The vehicle manufacturer specifies the pressure to which tyres on a vehicle should be inflated. This is the pressure that gives the best performance in road holding, efficient braking and fuel consumption. Most manufacturers specify different pressures for front and rear tyres.

A fault in what component would lead to uneven or excessive tyre wear?
Suspension. ABMW0698R

If a vehicle has a worn suspension it may lead to uneven or excessive tyre wear. If you notice that your tyres are unevenly worn, you should investigate the reason and have it repaired.

What can be affected by driving on under-inflated tyres?
Fuel consumption. ABMW0699R

Incorrect tyre pressure adversely affects many of a vehicle's systems, including brakes, suspension and steering. In particular, under-inflated tyres can increase the vehicle's fuel consumption.

When should tyre pressure be checked? ABMW0700R
When the tyres are cold.

You should check the tyre pressure in your vehicle once a week. Do this when the tyres are cold, using a reliable gauge. Tyres should always be inflated according to the vehicle manufacturer's guidelines.

What effect does low tyre-pressure have on a vehicle?
Braking and cornering are impaired. ABMW0701R

Incorrect tyre pressure adversely affects many of a vehicle's systems, including suspension, steering and fuel consumption. In particular, under-inflated tyres can affect the vehicle's braking ability and its effectiveness when cornering.

1

2

3

During a weekly check, a driver notices a badly worn front tyre. What should they do?
ABMW0702R

Have the worn tyre replaced.

The quality of the tyres on a vehicle is an important factor in the vehicle's road holding and braking ability. So if you notice that a tyre is badly worn, you should replace it as soon as possible. The minimum legal tread depth for tyres on most vehicles is 1.6mm, but you should replace a tyre before it becomes this worn.

What effect could hitting or mounting the kerb have on a vehicle's tyres?
It could damage the sidewalls.
ABMW0703R

If a vehicle hits or mounts the kerb it could damage the sidewall of the tyre. If that happens it could cause the tyre to 'blow-out' later. If this happens at high speed the vehicle could go out of control and crash.

What does worn tread along the edge of a tyre suggest?
ABMW0704R

Steering alignment may be faulty.

If you notice that a tyre on your vehicle is worn along its edge, this may indicate a problem with the steering. lignment. This is a potentially dangerous problem, and you should have it fixed as soon as possible.

What effect would under-inflated tyres have on a vehicle's transmission?
It would have no effect on it.
ABMW0705R

Incorrect tyre pressure adversely affects many of a vehicle's systems, including braking, suspension, steering and fuel consumption. It does not, however, affect the engine transmission.

What should a driver do before undertaking a long journey?
Check the tyres are inflated to normal air pressure.
ABMW0706R

It is important to check the tyre pressure before starting a long journey as incorrect air pressure can adversely affect many of the vehicles systems, including brakes, steering, suspension and fuel consumption.

Under what circumstances should a driver increase the air pressure in the tyres before undertaking a long journey? ABMW0707R
Never.

Check the air pressure before you start a long journey, and when you inflate the tyres, make sure that you follow the vehicle manufacturer's recommended tyre pressure This is the pressure that gives the best performance in road holding, efficient braking and fuel consumption.

What is the effect of under-inflated tyres on a vehicle? ABMW0708R
Impaired braking and steering.

Check the tyre pressure once a week. Incorrect tyre pressure adversely affects many of a vehicle's systems, including braking ability, suspension, steering and fuel consumption.

What effect would coasting have on a vehicle's tyres? ABMW0709R
No effect.

Coasting is a bad practice that happens when a driver allows a vehicle to move by its own momentum (or by gravity – for example, down a hill) with the engine disengaged. This can be done in two ways:

1. By putting the car into neutral gear while moving; or
2. By keeping the clutch pedal pressed down to disengage the selected gear.

If a vehicle is coasting, the driver has much less control, so you should never coast. However, it has no effect on the tyres.

What can be affected by driving on under-inflated tyres? ABMW27
Braking ability.

Incorrect tyre pressure adversely affects many of a vehicle's systems, including suspension, steering and fuel consumption. In particular, under-inflated tyres can affect the vehicle's braking ability.

1

2

3

What should the driver do to secure the vehicle when changing a wheel?

Ensure that the vehicle cannot roll when jacked up.   ABMW0710R

If you have to change a wheel, make sure you do it in a safe place on level ground. Also, apply the handbrake and engage a low gear to secure the vehicle before you jack it up.

While driving, what does a continuous vibration in the steering indicate?

The wheel balance is uneven.   ABMW0713R

If you feel a continuous vibration in the steering, particularly at higher speeds, this could indicate that the balance of the vehicle wheels is uneven. If this is the case, you should have it investigated by a mechanic.

What can cause heavy steering?

Under-inflated tyres.   ABMW0714R

Heavy steering is when you need to use more effort than usual to turn the steering wheel. You might experience this if the power-assisted steering system is not working properly, or more commonly, if the front tyres are under-inflated.

Clutch

In vehicles with manual transmission, the clutch enables the driver to disengage the engine from the transmission. This allows the engine to continue running while the vehicle is stopped, and makes it easy for the driver to change gears. In a car, the clutch is generally operated by the left-most pedal; on a motorcycle it is operated by a lever on the left handlebar.

Between the extremes of fully engaged and fully disengaged, the clutch transmits a varying proportion of the engine's force to the transmission, but it becomes very hot, and if you over-use the clutch it can become damaged ('burnt out'). For this reason you should avoid driving for long periods with the clutch partially engaged.

When driving, where should a driver rest their left foot?

On the floor or foot rest.   ABMW0711R

The clutch is the connection between the engine and the gearbox. It enables the vehicle to move when a gear is engaged. You should not rest your foot on the clutch pedal because it may disengage the selected gear or damage the clutch mechanism.

Environmental matters

Motor vehicles are a significant cause of pollution. All drivers should be aware of this, and should modify their driving habits to minimise their negative impact on the environment.

1
2
3

Minimising environmental impact

The questions in this section check that you understand environmental issues about driving, and you know how to drive in an environmentally responsible manner.

In what way do motor vehicles harm the environment?
By increasing carbon monoxide levels. ABMW0725R

Carbon monoxide is a poisonous gas emitted by vehicle exhausts into the atmosphere. Driving economically and keeping a vehicle well maintained can reduce the level of carbon monoxide emissions.

What can drivers do to help protect the environment? ABMW269
Car share.

Car sharing helps the environment. Drivers should consider car sharing for routine journeys for work or for the school run. This will reduce pollution and reduce traffic congestion at peak times.

What can be achieved by the driving style known as 'Eco-Driving'?
Reduced fuel consumption. ABMW0730R

The advantages of 'eco-driving' include improved road safety, improved fuel consumption and reduced emissions. The eco-conscious driver becomes a more efficient driver because they learn to read the road further ahead and display better anticipation skills. This reduces the need for harsh acceleration and braking which results in a more economical style of driving and a smoother drive.

What can be achieved by the driving style known as 'Eco-Driving'?
Increased road safety.

ABMW279

The advantages of 'eco-driving' include improved road safety, improved fuel consumption and reduced emissions. The eco-conscious driver becomes a more efficient driver because they learn to read the road further ahead and display better anticipation skills. This reduces the need for harsh acceleration and braking which results in a more economical style of driving and a smoother drive.

What can be achieved by the driving style known as 'Eco-Driving'?
Reduced emissions.

ABMW28

The advantages of 'eco-driving' include improved road safety, improved fuel consumption and reduced emissions. The eco-conscious driver becomes a more efficient driver because they learn to read the road further ahead and display better anticipation skills. This reduces the need for harsh acceleration and braking which results in a more economical style of driving and a smoother drive.

Which action contributes to Eco-Driving?
Maintaining a steady speed.

ABMW29

Eco-driving' contributes to road safety and also reduces fuel consumption and harmful emissions. Eco drivers will read the road well in advance and avoid harsh acceleration and late braking. Driving smoothly and maintaining a steady speed saves fuel and reduces wear and tear on vehicles.

Which action contributes to Eco-Driving?
Selecting a high gear as soon as possible.

ABMW0731R

Eco-driving' contributes to road safety and also reduces fuel consumption and harmful emissions. Eco-conscious drivers will read the road well in advance and avoid harsh acceleration and braking. Fuel consumption can be reduced by using the highest gear possible without causing the engine to labour.

Which action contributes to Eco-Driving?
Looking ahead and anticipating.

ABMW30

Eco-driving' contributes to road safety and also reduces fuel consumption and harmful emissions. Eco drivers read the road well ahead and anticipate what is going to happen in front. This reduces the need for harsh acceleration and braking which results in a more comfortable and safer drive while saving fuel and reducing emissions.

How can a driver help the environment?   ABMW0732R
By reducing speed.

As a driver you can do less damage to the environment if you drive smoothly and avoid harsh acceleration and braking. Vehicles travelling at 110 km/h use up to 30% more fuel than those travelling at 80km/h. However, you should not drive so slow as to inconvenience other road users.

Fuel consumption

Driving in such a way that you minimise your consumption of fuel is good for you and it's good for the planet. It saves you money, it uses less of a scarce resource, and it produces less pollution. It is also safer. These questions check that you know how to maximise your fuel efficiency.

1

2

3

What can a driver do to maximise fuel efficiency while driving?   ABMW0727R
Avoid carrying unnecessary weight.

The more extra weight is in your vehicle, the more fuel you use. Using a roof rack or a roof box increases wind resistance and this also increases fuel consumption – by as much as 15%. Remove roof racks and roof boxes when not in use.

Which action is likely to cause an increase in fuel consumption?   ABMW0728R
Harsh acceleration

Harsh acceleration increases fuel consumption. Driving smoothly reduces wear and tear and also improves fuel consumption. Use the highest gear possible without causing the engine to labour.

What alternatives can drivers take to help protect the environment?
Use public transport.   ABMW0729R

Using public transport helps to protect the environment. Buses, trams and trains are a more environmentally friendly way to move large numbers of people especially in urban areas. Consider using public transport where possible – not only is it more environmentally friendly, but it can also be more cost-effective when you take the cost of fuel and parking charges into ount.

What should a driver do to minimise fuel consumption in their vehicle?
Use gentle acceleration and braking.

ABMW0716R

Driving smoothly will help reduce your fuel consumption. Read the road ahead and adjust your speed in good time, and avoid harsh acceleration and late braking.

How does harsh acceleration affect fuel consumption?
ABMW0715

Fuel consumption increases.

Harsh acceleration increases fuel consumption, and driving smoothly helps to reduce your fuel consumption and the emissions from your vehicle. Try not to over-rev the engine and use the appropriate gear for the speed of the vehicle. When slowing down, take your foot off the accelerator and allow the vehicle to slow progressively before you brake.

How does continuous high-speed driving affect fuel consumption?
It increases fuel consumption.

ABMW0717R

Driving at high speeds increases your fuel consumption. A vehicle travelling at 112km/h uses approximately 30% more fuel than one travelling at 80km/h.

1

2

3

What should a driver do to ensure better fuel efficiency from their vehicle?
ABMW0718R
Ensure that the vehicle is regularly serviced.

One of the keys to good fuel efficiency is making sure that your vehicle is well maintained. Servicing should be carried out as recommended by the manufacturer. Checking the tyre pressure regularly can also help ensure good fuel efficiency.

How can fuel efficiency be improved?
ABMW0719R
By using gentle acceleration and making gear changes appropriate to speed.

The way you drive can contribute to your vehicle's fuel efficiency:
Accelerate gently;
Use the highest available gear (without causing the engine to struggle); and
Drive smoothly – this also reduces wear and tear on a vehicle.

Noise

Motor vehicles make a lot of noise. You should try to make sure that your vehicle and your style of driving do not create so much noise that they cause a nuisance to others.

What effect does a worn exhaust have on a vehicle?
ABMW0720R

It causes noise and gas pollution levels to increase.

A vehicle with a worn exhaust will probably be noisier and will produce more polluting emissions. There are strict regulations governing the noise and emission levels of vehicles, and these are rigorously checked during a vehicle's NCT.

Is a driver allowed to sound the horn while driving in a built-up area at night?
ABMW0721R

Yes, but between 11:30pm and 7:00am the horn may be sounded only in an emergency.

You are not allowed to use the horn in a built-up area between 11:30pm and 7:00am unless there is a traffic emergency. Only use a horn to warn other road users of oncoming danger or if you need to make them aware of your presence for safety reasons. Using the horn does not give you an automatic right of way. Never use the horn to provoke a reaction from or to rebuke another motorist.

Under what circumstances is it permitted to replace the standard horn on a vehicle with a musical horn?
ABMW0722

Never.

A horn is designed to be an audible warning device. You should not make any technical modifications to the horn without professional advice as these may have legal and safety implications.

When is the use of the horn prohibited?
ABMW0723R

Between 11:30pm and 7:00am in a built-up area.

You are not allowed to use the horn in a built-up area between 11:30pm and 7:00am unless there is a traffic emergency. Only use a horn to warn other road users of oncoming danger or if you need to make them aware of your presence for safety reasons. Using the horn does not give you an automatic right of way. Never use the horn to provoke a reaction from or to rebuke another motorist.

Taking corrective or emergency action

When you are driving, you need to always expect the unexpected. You literally don't know what's around the next bend, but you can avoid some dangerous situations by developing your observation skills and learning to anticipate danger. Even the best and safest drivers, however, will have to take corrective or emergency actions from time to time.

1
2
3

Skidding

You should always drive in a way that is suited to the weather conditions and the state of the road. If you do, you will generally avoid skidding. However, if you do find yourself in a skid, you must know how to react in order to get the vehicle back into control as soon as possible. These questions check that you understand the causes of skidding and how to avoid them.

What can cause a vehicle to skid?
ABMW0733R

Using harsh acceleration.

Using harsh acceleration at the wrong time can cause a vehicle to skid, especially if the road is wet.

What can cause a vehicle to skid?
ABMW31

Excessive heavy braking.

Heavy braking can cause a vehicle to skid, particularly if the road surface is wet or uneven, or if the tyres are worn or incorrectly inflated. Read the road well ahead and try to avoid heavy braking, particularly in wet or slippery conditions.

What can cause a vehicle to skid?
ABMW32

Excessive speed.

Excessive speed can result in a vehicle going into a skid. You should always drive at a safe speed and never exceed the speed limit for the road you are on. Excessive speed is particularly dangerous in wet and slippery conditions.

Punctures

A puncture is always an inconvenience, but it is also sometimes dangerous. If you get a sudden puncture while driving, you must know what to do in order to keep control of the vehicle and not endanger yourself or others.

What should a driver do if a front tyre bursts? ABMW0605R
Grip the steering wheel firmly.

If a front tyre bursts on a vehicle, the steering on the vehicle will become unstable. Don't panic – slow down gradually while keeping a firm hold on the steering wheel. Stop in a safe place to change the wheel, and alert other road users by switching on your hazard warning lights.

What should a driver do if their vehicle gets a puncture on a motorway?
Pull in where safe on the hard shoulder and call for assistance. ABMW0606R

Don't try to change a wheel on a motorway, as this could be very dangerous. Drive the car on to the hard shoulder, and when it is safe to do so, get out of the vehicle and move behind the barrier. Call for assistance from a motorway emergency phone or using a mobile phone (call the Gardaí).

1
2
3

Fire

Fire in a vehicle is rare, but if it does occur it can be very dangerous, both for the people in the vehicle and for others in the vicinity. You should know the precautions to take against fire, and know what to do if fire does break out in your vehicle.

What precautions could a driver take against the risk of fire in their vehicle?

ABMW0607R

Investigate strong fumes and carry a fire extinguisher.

A strong smell of fuel is usually an indication that something is wrong, and you should stop and investigate as soon as possible. Leaking or spilling petrol can be dangerous because it is so combustible. It is good practice to carry a fire extinguisher in your vehicle, so that you can deal with any small fires.

Breakdowns

If your vehicle breaks down, you should make sure that it does not cause a hazard to other road users, and that any action you take does not put you or others in danger.

When should a driver use hazard warning lights on a motorway?

When the vehicle has broken down.

ABMW0609R

If your vehicle breaks down on a motorway, drive it to the hard shoulder and switch on the hazard warning lights to warn following traffic. When it is safe to do so, get out of the vehicle and move behind the barrier. Call for assistance from a motorway emergency phone or using a mobile phone (call the Gardaí).

What should a driver do if their vehicle is broken down and they are awaiting assistance?

ABMW0610

Switch on the vehicle hazard warning lights, get out of the vehicle and stand to the side.

If your vehicle breaks down on the road, always switch on the hazard warning lights and stand clear of the vehicle while awaiting assistance – this will warn other traffic that there is a vehicle stopped on the road.

Meeting emergency or extra-large vehicles

It is important that you know how to react and respond when you meet emergency vehicles, such as fire brigades, ambulances and Garda cars, either coming towards you or coming up behind you. These vehicles are sometimes moving very fast, and you must get out of their way as quickly as you can, provided it is safe to do so.

What action should a driver take when they notice flashing blue lights in the rear-view mirror?   ABMW0734R

Move to the left, reduce speed and allow the vehicle to pass.

When you notice an emergency vehicle in the rear-view mirror, you should move into the left where it is safe and allow the vehicle to pass safely. Avoid stopping immediately as this could cause a greater obstruction to the emergency vehicle.

What should a driver do when they see road works machinery with amber flashing lights up ahead?   ABMW0735R

Slow down and prepare to stop if necessary.

When you notice works vehicles ahead, slow down and be prepared to stop for the road works. Be extra careful driving through road works as the road surface could be uneven or slippery.

What action should a driver take when they meet a vehicle with flashing blue lights.   ABMW0736R

Move to the left, reduce speed and stop if necessary.

When a driver notices an emergency vehicle approaching in the distance, they should check their mirror and move to the left to allow the vehicle to pass. On some occasions it may be necessary to stop.

What should a driver do if an ambulance is stopped up ahead with its flashing blue lights on?   ABMW0737

Reduce speed and prepare to stop if necessary.

When you come upon an emergency vehicle stopped on the road, you should slow down and be prepared to stop. Do not stop to see what is happening as this could be dangerous and you might cause an obstruction to the flow of traffic.

1
2
3

How are emergency vehicles identified?
ABMW0738R

By flashing red or blue lights.

If you hear or see an emergency vehicle approaching sounding its siren or flashing lights, be extra careful and give way if it is safe to do so.

Which vehicle is exempt from speed limits when being used in an emergency?
ABMW0739R

Fire brigade.

In the course of their duty Gardai, Fire Brigade and ambulance personnel are exempt from some traffic laws including speed limits, as long as they do not put other road users in danger. If you hear or see a Garda or emergency vehicle approaching under emergency conditions, be extra careful and give way, if it is safe to do so.

Which vehicle is exempt from speed limits when being used in an emergency?
ABMW33

Ambulance.

In the course of their duty Gardai, Fire Brigade and ambulance personnel are exempt from some traffic laws including speed limits, as long as they do not put other road users in danger. If you hear or see a Garda or emergency vehicle approaching under emergency conditions, be extra careful and give way, if it is safe to do so.

Which vehicle is exempt from speed limits when being used in an emergency?
ABMW34

Garda.

In the course of their duty Gardai, Fire Brigade and ambulance personnel are exempt from some traffic laws including speed limits, as long as they do not put other road users in danger. If you hear or see a Garda or emergency vehicle approaching under emergency conditions, be extra careful and give way, if it is safe to do so.

Section 2
Cars, light vans, tractors and works vehicles

1
2
3

Alert driving and showing consideration for other road users

1
2
3

When you are driving, you need to always expect the unexpected. You literally don't know what's around the next bend, but you can avoid some dangerous situations by developing your observation skills and learning to anticipate danger. Even the best and safest drivers, however, will have to take corrective or emergency actions from time to time.

What should a driver do when they want to use a mobile phone?
Pull in and stop in a safe place. BW0001R

It is illegal to use a mobile phone while driving. Driving requires all of your attention, all of the time, so you should never use a mobile phone while on the road. If you want to use a mobile phone, you should find a safe place to stop.

When parked on a busy road, what should the driver be aware of? BW0002R
Before opening the door the driver should make sure it is safe to do so.

When you park a vehicle on a busy road, make sure it is safe before opening the door, as there could be traffic passing close by.

In this situation, what should the driver in the right-hand lane of the dual carriageway be aware of? BW0004R
Crosswinds may blow the rider into their path.

In wet and windy conditions a driver should be aware of vulnerable road users being blown into their path. Always expect the unexpected.

1
2
3

Seeing where you are going

1
2
3

As a driver, you must be able to see where you are going, and you must adjust the way you are driving to suit the road, weather and traffic conditions all around you. When you are going forward, you will mainly use your windscreen and mirrors for this; when you are reversing you will mainly be looking over your shoulder, while glancing around frequently.

Making sure that you can see properly

While you are driving any motor vehicle, you must have a clear view of the road ahead, and you must also be constantly aware of the road and traffic conditions around you to the sides and rear. The questions in this section check that you understand the importance of this, and that you know how to react if your view is obstructed in any way.

What should a driver do before towing a caravan? BW0005R
Have extended mirrors fitted to the towing vehicle and use them regularly.

If you intend towing a caravan that is wider than the vehicle that is towing it, you should fit extended mirrors to both sides of the towing vehicle, so that you will be able to assess the traffic situation behind and to the sides.

What should a driver do before towing a wide-bodied trailer? BW0006R
Make use of extended mirrors to check for following traffic.

If you intend towing a trailer that is wider or higher than the vehicle that is towing it, you should fit extended mirrors to both sides of the towing vehicle, so that you will be able to assess the traffic situation behind and to the sides.

Why is it important to have clean, clear windows? BW0007R
To ensure good all round visibility from the vehicle.

Make sure the windows of your vehicle are clear and clean at all times so that you can see road and traffic conditions around you. Dirty windows are particularly hazardous when the sun is low and at night.

If the vehicle's windows are covered with ice, what should the driver do before undertaking a journey? BW0008R
Clear the ice from the windows before starting.

Make sure the windows of your vehicle are clear and clean at all times so that you can see road and traffic conditions around you. This is especially important when driving in slippery conditions. It is good practice to carry a can of de-icer in the vehicle and if possible to fill the washer reservoir with a de-icing agent.

1
2
3

What should a driver do if the vehicle's windows are covered in ice?
Switch on the heating system and use a scraper to clear the ice before driving. BW0009R

Make sure the windows of your vehicle are clear and clean at all times so that you can see road and traffic conditions around you. This is especially important when driving in slippery conditions. It is good practice to carry a can of de-icer in the vehicle and if possible to fill the washer reservoir with a de-icing agent.

What should a driver do if condensation is affecting the vehicle's windows? BW0010R
Dry the windows with a cloth and then use the demister system.

Make sure the windows of your vehicle are clear and clean at all times so that you can see road and traffic conditions around you. Condensation on the window can seriously impair your ability to make proper observations.

How can sunlight affect visibility in a car with grimy windows? BW0011R
It can create a mirror effect and reduce visibility.

Make sure the windows of your vehicle are clear and clean at all times so that you can see road and traffic conditions around you. Dirty windows are a particular hazard when the sun is low in the sky and at night.

Reversing

When you are reversing a vehicle, your ability to see where you are going and to see around the vehicle is restricted. For this reason, you must check carefully before you start, and execute the manoeuve slowly and carefully, checking all around you as you go. The questions in this section check your understanding of this issue.

What specific observations should a driver make before reversing their vehicle?
BW0012R
Look over both shoulders and behind.

Before reversing, look over both shoulders and to the rear to check that there are no children or other road users around the vehicle and that it is safe to reverse.

What specific observations should a driver make before reversing a vehicle fitted with an audible warning device?
BW0013
Observations should be made to the front, sides and rear of the vehicle, including blind spots.

Before reversing, make sure it is safe to do so by taking all appropriate observations to the front, sides and rear of the vehicle, including the blind spots. Never assume it is safe to reverse just because the vehicle has an audible warning device.

What should a driver do when they intend to reverse onto a side road?
Check carefully all around before and during the reverse.
BW0014R

Before reversing onto a side road, check all around to make sure it is safe and clear to carry out the manoeuvre, paying particular attention to pedestrians crossing behind the vehicle and any other approaching traffic.

What should a driver do when they intend to reverse their vehicle on a busy street?
BW0015R
Reverse slowly, checking all around for other road users.

When reversing on a busy street, look all around and reverse slowly because there may be passing traffic and pedestrians attempting to cross the road.

1
2
3

What should a driver do if they intend to reverse their vehicle into an area which they cannot see?
BW0016R

Ask someone to assist when reversing.

Do not attempt to reverse into an area that you cannot see into properly, unless you get assistance from somebody who can advise you when it is safe to do so.

What should a driver do when reversing a vehicle with a trailer attached?
BW0017R

Look all around and use rear-view mirrors when reversing.

When reversing a vehicle with a trailer attached, make sure it is safe by checking all around and using the vehicle's mirrors. Reversing a vehicle with a trailer attached requires a lot of concentration, so watch out for other road users in the vicinity.

Remaining alert

Every driver has a responsibility to remain alert, and not to do anything that might impair their ability to react and respond to changes in the road or traffic conditions, or to the actions of other road users. Drivers should also be aware of the capabilities and limitations of the vehicle they are driving, and not drive in such a way that they endanger themselves or others.

What should a driver do in order to keep alert during a long journey?
Increase the air circulation and make regular stops if necessary. BW0018R

While on a long journey, you should take regular rest breaks. A short walk and a caffeinated drink (tea or coffee) can help to revive you. Keep the vehicle cool and well ventilated with a steady flow of fresh air.

What would be the effect of a warm vehicle interior on somebody driving at night?
BW0019R

It could make the driver feel drowsy.

If you are driving at night in a vehicle with a high interior temperature, you can become drowsy. Keep the interior of the vehicle cool and well ventilated, and take regular breaks.

What effect would exhaust gases leaking into a vehicle have on the driver?

BW0020R

The driver may become drowsy or ill.

Exhaust gases leaking into a vehicle can make the driver drowsy or ill, and this can lead to a serious collision. If you suspect that exhaust gases are leaking into the vehicle, you should have it checked by a qualified person.

What in particular should a driver be aware of when driving a high-powered vehicle?

BW0021R

It could make the driver feel they are driving slower than they actually are.

When driving a smooth, high-powered vehicle, you may have the impression that you are travelling slower than you actually are. You should always know the speed at which you are driving, and adjust it as necessary to suit the road and traffic conditions.

Using the handbrake

Before you drive any vehicle, you must be familiar with its features and controls, and you must know how and when to use them. One of the most important features of any vehicle is its braking systems, and you must know when it is appropriate to use the foot brake and when to use the handbrake.

When should the handbrake be used to bring a vehicle to a halt?

BW0024R

Never.

The handbrake should never be used to bring a vehicle to a halt. This practice is potentially dangerous, as the rear wheels could lock up and the vehicle could skid out of control. In addition, using the handbrake does not operate the rear brake lights to warn following traffic.

What is the danger associated with applying the handbrake at speed?

The back wheels could lock and cause the vehicle to skid.

BW0025R

The handbrake should never be used when travelling at speed. This practice is potentially dangerous, as the rear wheels could lock up and the vehicle could skid out of control.

1

2

3

Driving on different road surfaces

You must modify your driving behaviour to take account of changes in the weather, the traffic conditions and the road surfaces. The questions in this section check that you know how to respond to different road surfaces.

In slippery conditions, should the driver of a tractor use the grass verge to improve road holding?
BW0022R
No, using the grass verge should be avoided.

You should not use the grass verge to gain traction on slippery roads. Hidden gulleys in the verge could cause you to lose control.

Why should a tractor be driven more slowly on uneven road surfaces?
To avoid severe bouncing.
BW0023R

Driving a tractor at speed on an uneven road surface could cause the vehicle or the trailer to become unstable and difficult to control.

Driving in fog

Driving in fog can be difficult, tiring and dangerous. Not only do you have difficulty in seeing the road markings and other traffic, but other road users also have difficulty in seeing you. The questions in this section check that you understand this issue and know how to respond.

When should rear fog lights be used?
In dense fog or falling snow.
BW0026R

You should use your rear fog lights only in fog or falling snow. Using fog lights in normal road and weather conditions can dazzle or blind following motorists. Also, fog lights may make your brake lights harder to see.

When should high-intensity rear fog lights be used?
When driving in fog or falling snow.
BW0027R

You should use your rear fog lights only in fog or falling snow. Using fog lights in normal road and weather conditions can dazzle or blind following motorists. Also, fog lights may make your brake lights harder to see.

Driving at night

Driving at night, particularly along unlit roads or in wet weather, is challenging. You need to be sure that you can see the road ahead well enough, and that you can be seen by other road users.

What should a driver do if the right-hand headlight bulb fails when driving at night? BW0028R
Have the bulb replaced immediately.

Vehicles (except motorcycles) are required by law to have right and left headlights. Faulty lights should be repaired immediately. A vehicle with only one headlight can cause a hazard to other road users or be mistaken for a motorcycle.

What should a driver do if dazzled by headlights reflecting in the rear-view mirror of their car? BW0029R
Use the night driving mode on the mirror.

If the lights of following traffic are dazzling you, adjust your rear-view mirror to the night driving mode. This will allow you to concentrate on the road ahead and not be distracted by lights from following traffic.

What should a driver do if dazzled by lights reflecting in their exterior mirror? BW0030R
Temporarily adjust the angle of the mirror.

If the lights of following traffic reflecting in your exterior mirror are dazzling you, temporarily adjust the angle of the mirror to relieve the glare and allow you to drive without distraction.

At night, what effect could driving with a single headlight have on oncoming drivers? BW0031R
They could mistake the vehicle for a motorcycle.

Motor vehicles (except motorcycles) are required by law to have two headlights. A vehicle with only one headlight could be mistaken for a motorcycle and other road users could believe that it is in a different position on the road than it actually is. You must repair faulty lighting immediately.

1
2
3

Generally, what lighting must a car, tractor or works vehicle have when driving at night?
BW0032

Headlights, front and rear side lights, rear number plate light, red rear reflectors, brake lights and indicators.

Cars, tractors and works vehicles are required by law to have headlights, front and rear side lights, rear number plate light, rear reflectors, brake lights and indicators.

What lights must be shown on a parked car, tractor or works vehicle at night on an unlit public road?
BW0033

At least one side lamp front and rear on the side nearest the centre of the road.

When leaving a vehicle on an unlit public road at night you should leave side/parking lights on, so that your vehicle can be seen by other road users.

Bridges and tunnels

Before going under a bridge or entering a tunnel, you must make sure that your vehicle will fit under it. You will see a advance warning sign before you come to the bridge or tunnel specifying the maximum height of vehicle that it can accommodate.

In addition, going over some bridges – in particular humpback bridges – poses a particular hazard for vehicles pulling a trailer, as there is a danger that the trailer may become detached from the towing vehicle.

What danger could be associated with driving a tractor and trailer over a humpbacked bridge?
BW0034R

The trailer could become detached.

When towing a trailer, make sure that the tow hitch always has sufficient ground clearance. If this hits the road, for example when travelling over a humpbacked bridge, there is a danger that the trailer will become detached.

What should a driver do before entering a tunnel?
BW0035R

Check that the height of the vehicle is suitable for the tunnel.

You should know height of your vehicle and the load you are carrying, and plan your route accordingly. Always read the road ahead and watch for warning signs about height restrictions. These may relate to tunnels, low bridges or car park entrances.

What should a driver do before starting a journey on which they will encounter a tunnel?
BW0036R

Check the tunnel height before starting the journey.

You should know height of your vehicle and the load you are carrying, and plan your route accordingly. Always read the road ahead and watch for warning signs about height restrictions. These may relate to tunnels, low bridges or car park entrances.

Driving licences and learner permits

1

2

3

The questions in this section test that you know what the holder of each category of driving licence and learner permit is allowed and not allowed to do.

Where should L-plates be displayed on cars?
BW0037R

Both front and rear.

The holder of a learner permit must display L-plates on the front and rear of their car at all times when driving on public roads.

When must the holder of a Learner Permit display L-plates on their car?
At all times when driving.
BW0038R

The holder of a learner permit must display L-plates on the front and rear of their car at all times when driving on public roads.

How would a driver calculate the maximum permitted weight of their vehicle?
BW0039R

By adding the unladen weight of the vehicle to the load permitted to be carried.

The maximum permitted weight of a vehicle is the sum of the unladen weight of the vehicle and the maximum load that may be carried in it. It is an offence to overload a vehicle, as it reduces your ability to control it effectively.

What is the maximum gross weight of a vehicle that may be driven by the holder of a category B driving licence?
BW0040R

3,500 kilograms.

The holder of a category B driving licence is not permitted to drive a vehicle with a design gross vehicle weight of more than 3,500kgs. This restriction is noted on the licence.

What is the maximum number of passengers that may be carried in a vehicle driven by the holder of a category B driving licence?
BW0044R

8 passengers.

The holder of a category B driving licence is not permitted to drive a vehicle that has seating for more than 8 passengers excluding the driver.

When can the holder of a Category W Learner Permit carry a passenger?
Only when the passenger also holds a Category W driving licence and the vehicle is designed to take a passenger.
BW0045R

The holder of a category W learner permit may carry a passenger in the vehicle only if: the vehicle is designed to take a passenger, and the passenger has held a full driving licence in category W for two or more years.

Collisions and breakdowns

At the scene of a collision or breakdown, do not do anything that might make the situation worse. Make sure that any injured persons are properly attended to by contacting the emergency services. Make sure that oncoming traffic is given adequate warning of any hazard and that bystanders are not exposed to danger.

A driver has stalled in the middle of an unguarded level crossing and cannot restart the engine. The warning bell is ringing. What should the driver do? BW0046R

Walk clear of the crossing and phone the signal operator so that trains can be stopped.

In this situation, you and all passengers should get out of the vehicle and immediately use the emergency phone at the crossing to contact the signal operator so that trains can be stopped. If necessary, warn other motorists. Do not return to the vehicle until instructed by the signal operator or emergency services.

1
2
3

What should a driver do if their vehicle breaks down on an automatic railway level crossing? BW0051R

Get passengers clear of the crossing and phone the signal operator so that trains can be stopped.

In this situation, you and all passengers should get out of the vehicle and immediately use the emergency phone at the crossing to contact the signal operator so that trains can be stopped. If necessary, warn other motorists. Do not return to the vehicle until instructed by the signal operator or emergency services.

What is the immediate effect of a head-on collision between two cars at speed? BW0053

All persons in each vehicle are thrown violently forward.

In a head-on collision passengers in both vehicles are propelled forwards, and if they are not wearing seatbelts they may go through the windscreen. It is the driver's responsibility to ensure that all passengers under the age of 17 wear seatbelts. Older passengers are themselves responsible for wearing seatbelts.

When changing a wheel on a public road, what should a person do to ensure their own safety? BW0055R

Wear reflective clothing and switch on the vehicle hazard warning lights.

When changing a wheel at the side of the road, switch on the vehicle hazard warning lights, and wear reflective or light-coloured clothing. This will help other motorists to react and slow down when passing.

Carrying passengers

The questions in this section check that you know the regulations relating to carrying passengers, and that you know how to drive and operate your vehicle in a way that ensures the comfort and safety of the passengers.

Why is it dangerous to allow children to stand in the space between the front seats of a car? BW0047R

They could be thrown forward if the brakes are applied suddenly.

When carrying children in a car or goods vehicle, it is the driver's responsibility to make sure that they are suitably restrained.

When are children allowed to stand with their heads up through an open sun roof? BW0048R

Children are never allowed to do so.

When carrying children in a car or goods vehicle, it is the driver's responsibility to make sure that they are suitably restrained.

When may the holder of a Category W Learner Permit carry a passenger on a tractor or works vehicle? BW0049

When there is proper passenger seating and the passenger holds a full category W licence.

The holder of a category W licence may carry a passenger in the vehicle only if: 1.the vehicle is designed to take a passenger, and 2. the passenger has held a full driving licence in category W for two or more years.

Are children allowed to be left unattended in a vehicle? BW0050R
Children should never be left unattended in a vehicle.

Children must not be left unattended in a vehicle, even for a short period of time. Children might interfere with the vehicle's controls, and would not be able to deal with an emergency situation, such as a fire or electrical malfunction which could result in serious injury or death.

When is a driver allowed to carry more passengers in a car than there are seat belts available? BW0056R
It is never allowed.

A driver must make sure that each passenger in the vehicle has a seatbelt. Failure to wear a seatbelt is an offence. It is the driver's responsibility to ensure that passengers under the age of 17 wear seatbelts. Older passengers are themselves responsible for wearing seatbelts.

Safety on tractors

The questions in this section check that you understand the dangers of working in or around tractors.

When should children be allowed to drive a tractor? BW0052R
Children should never be allowed to drive a tractor.

Persons under 16 years of age are not permitted to drive a tractor in a public place.

What danger can arise from the power take-off shaft of a tractor? BW0054
If it is not covered, clothing can get caught in it.

If you are working at the rear of a tractor, you should bear in mind that if the power take-off shaft is not covered, loose clothing might get caught in it and lead to injury or death.

Carrying loads

The questions in this section check that you know the dangers associated with carrying a load in your vehicle, and that you know how to do so safely.

What should a driver do when requested to drive a vehicle that they feel is overloaded?
BW0057R
Refuse to drive the vehicle.

You should not take a vehicle that you believe to be overloaded onto a public road. Overloading is dangerous, as it affects the stability and braking capabilities of the vehicle.

How could towing an overloaded trailer affect a vehicle?
BW0058R
It could impair the vehicle's steering and braking.

You should not take an overloaded trailer onto a public road. An overloaded trailer impairs the stability, steering and braking of the towing vehicle.

When is a red flag a sufficient marker for a rear load overhang that exceeds one metre?
BW0129R
Only during the day.

During daylight hours, you must use a red flag to mark any load that is protruding more than one metre. At night, you must use a red light.

At what point is a vehicle load more likely to shift?
BW0130R
When cornering.

It is the driver's responsibility to ensure that the load is properly secured and evenly distributed, so that the vehicle can be properly controlled when changing direction and when braking.

How should a driver negotiate a bend when driving a fully loaded vehicle?
BW0131R
At a slower speed than when empty.

Driving too fast on the approach to a bend and while driving through it with a fully loaded vehicle can lead to a loss of control. This can be prevented by driving in a safe and sensible manner and by reading the road ahead.

Towing a trailer

The questions in this section check that you know how to tow a trailer safely.

When attaching a trailer to their vehicle, what should a driver check?
That the load is evenly spread. BW0060R

Proper weight distribution helps to ensure the stability of both the towing vehicle and the trailer. In the trailer, the bulk of the load should be over the axles. If a heavy load is positioned at the front of the trailer, this will result in too much 'nose weight' on the hitch of the towing vehicle and make it difficult to steer. If a heavy load is positioned at the rear of the trailer, this will result in reduced weight on the rear axle of the towing vehicle, which will make it more unstable.

When attaching a trailer to their vehicle, what should a driver check?
That the trailer coupling is attached securely. BW0061R

Before towing a trailer or a caravan, check that the tow bar is securely attached to the towing vehicle, that the trailer coupling is properly attached to the tow bar and locked in place, and that the breakaway cable is properly connected.

1
2
3

What should a driver do to secure the towing vehicle before unhitching a trailer?
Apply the handbrake, switch off the ignition and engage a low gear. BW0062R

Before unhitching a trailer, apply the handbrake, switch off the ignition and engage a lower gear, so that the towing vehicle does not move while you are unhitching the trailer.

When is it permissible for a driver to carry a passenger on a trailer drawbar?
Never. BW0063R

You must never carry a passenger on a trailer drawbar because of the danger of the passenger falling between the vehicle and the trailer and being seriously injured or killed.

When is a tractor most likely to overturn?

BW0064R

When turning sharply.

When you are driving a tractor, you should be aware that tractors are less stable than other vehicles and take extra care when manoeuvring.

When driving a tractor and trailer, what should the driver do on entering a roundabout to avoid possible roll-over?

BW0065R

Reduce speed.

When you are driving a tractor with a trailer, you need to take extra care because of the vehicle's instability. Always drive at a safe speed, in particular when changing direction, such as on a roundabout.

What is jack-knifing?

BW0066R

When the trailer is travelling faster than the drawing vehicle.

Towing a trailer or caravan dramatically reduces the stability of the towing vehicle. If a driver brakes sharply or slows down quickly, the trailer may pivot around the tow hitch coupling, causing both vehicles to go off course, and possibly overturn.

When is jack-knifing most likely to occur?

BW0067

When trying to reduce speed sharply while travelling downhill.

Towing a trailer or caravan dramatically reduces the stability of the towing vehicle. If a driver brakes sharply or slows down quickly, the trailer may pivot around the tow hitch coupling, causing both vehicles to go off course, and possibly overturn.

The driver of a tractor pulling a wide load that blocks their view to the rear wishes to turn right. What should they do?

BW0068R

Have another person advise of following traffic while the driver checks for oncoming traffic.

If you are driving a vehicle with a wide load that blocks your view of the road to the rear, and you need to turn right, you should get someone else to look out to the rear and advise you when it is safe to make the turn.

Technical matters with a bearing on road safety

1
2
3

The questions in this section check that you know how to keep your vehicle in good condition, that you recognise signs that it needs to be repaired or serviced, and that you understand the implications for your own safety and that of others of driving a vehicle in poor condition.

Side lights

The primary purpose of side lights is to make the vehicle more visible when it is parked. Don't use them when driving at night – use dipped headlights instead.

When should a driver use the vehicle side lights? BW0069R
When parking on an unlit road.

You should use the side lights of your vehicle when parking on an unlit road at night, so that the vehicle can be easily seen by other road users.

How does a driver know if the bulb in a side light has failed? BW0070R
By checking the side lights when they are switched on.

You must ensure that the lights in your vehicle are working properly before driving on the road. Check all the vehicle lights regularly by switching them on and getting out of the vehicle to see if they are working, or by getting someone else to check for you.

Dashboard warning lights

Modern engines are equipped with sophisticated systems for monitoring the condition of the engine and other parts of the vehicle, and for warning the driver if something goes wrong. These warnings are generally in the form of a warning light on the dashboard.

What does this warning light indicate?
A fault in the braking system.

BW0154R

If the brake warning light is on, there is a problem with the braking system in the vehicle or the handbrake is on. You should not drive the vehicle until the problem has been rectified.

Lights on trailers

If you are towing a trailer, it must have a rear number plate. The lighting requirements are similar to those for the towing vehicle. These questions check that you know these requirements.

What lighting should be on a car-trailer?   BW0077R

Indicators, brake lights, rear number plate light, red reflectors and rear tail lights.

All vehicles, including trailers, must have rear indicators, brake lights, a rear number plate light, red reflectors and rear tail lights.

What lighting should be on a tractor-trailer during lighting-up hours?

Indicators, brake lights, rear number plate light, red reflectors and rear tail lights.   BW0078

All vehicles, including trailers, must have rear indicators, brake lights, a rear number plate light, red reflectors and rear tail lights.

1

2

3

Hazard warning lights

Your hazard warning lights are an important way of communicating to other road users that there is a danger on the road ahead. You should know when and how to use them.

On a motorway, when should a driver use the hazard warning lights?

When slowing down quickly because of danger ahead.   BW0071R

Use the hazard warning lights to warn other road users of a danger ahead. For example, if you have to slow down sharply because of a build-up of traffic ahead, you can use the hazard warning lights to warn following vehicles that they need to slow down.

What effect do the hazard warning lights have on the brake lights?

They have no effect.   BW0072R

Use the hazard warning lights to warn other road users of a danger ahead, when your vehicle is broken down and causing an obstruction, or when you needs to slow down sharply on a motorway. The hazard lights work independently of the other lights on the vehicle (except the direction indicators), and have no effect on the brake lights.

When should a driver use their hazard warning lights?

BW0073R

When the vehicle has broken down.

Use the hazard warning lights to warn other road users of a danger ahead. For example, if your vehicle has broken down and is stopped on the hard shoulder, you can use the hazard warning lights to warn following vehicles of your presence.

What does using the vehicle's hazard warning lights allow a driver to do?

To warn other road users that the vehicle is broken down.

BW0074R

Use the hazard warning lights to warn other road users of a danger ahead, when your vehicle is broken down and causing an obstruction, or when you needs to slow down sharply on a motorway.

When should a driver use their vehicle's hazard warning lights?

When causing an unavoidable obstruction.

BW0075R

Use the hazard warning lights to warn other road users of a danger ahead, when your vehicle is broken down and causing an obstruction, or when you needs to slow down sharply on a motorway.

When should a driver use their vehicle's hazard warning lights?

When broken down and causing an obstruction.

BW0076R

Use the hazard warning lights to warn other road users of a danger ahead, when your vehicle is broken down and causing an obstruction, or when you needs to slow down sharply on a motorway.

On a motorway, when should a driver use the hazard warning lights?

When the vehicle has broken down.

BW1

Use the hazard warning lights to warn other road users of a danger ahead. For example, if your vehicle has broken down and is stopped on the hard shoulder, you can use the hazard warning lights to warn following vehicles of your presence.

Brakes

Before you drive any vehicle, you must be familiar with its features and controls, and you must know how and when to use them. One of the most important features of any vehicle is its braking systems, and you must know when it is appropriate to use the foot brake and when to use the handbrake.

The handbrake generally works on which wheels? BW0079R
The rear wheels.

The function of the handbrake (or 'parking brake') is to stop the vehicle from moving when it is parked or when it is stopped on a hill. You normally use the handbrake when the vehicle is already stationary – you don't use it to stop the vehicle. It is even more important to use the handbrake when parked on a hill or when stationary in a vehicle with automatic transmission to prevent creep. In most vehicles, the handbrake operates on the rear wheels only.

In general, above what gross vehicle weight must a trailer have brakes fitted? BW0080R
750 kg

Brakes must be fitted to a trailer if its gross vehicle weight exceeding 750kg or half the weight of the towing vehicle.

Driving a vehicle with automatic transmission

A vehicle with automatic transmission has some obvious differences from one with manual transmission (such as no clutch), and some differences that are not so obvious. You need to be aware of these differences, particularly if you sometimes drive a manual vehicle and sometimes an automatic.

What is the recommended method of driving a vehicle with automatic transmission? BW0081R
Operate the accelerator and brake with the right foot.

When driving an automatic vehicle, you should use the right foot to operate both the accelerator and the brake, just as in vehicles with a manual gear box.

1

2

3

Fuel and oil

The oil in your engine lubricates and cools the moving parts of the engine. If there is too little oil in the engine, or if it is not reaching the parts that need it, the engine can be permanently damaged. Over-filling the engine with oil also causes problems.

If you are driving a diesel engined car, you must always use unrebated (white) diesel in it, rather than green diesel.

When driving a vehicle with a diesel engine in freezing weather, what should a driver ensure?
BW0082R

That the fuel is treated with an anti-waxing agent.

Road diesel is supplied with an anti-waxing agent added to it. This generally prevents the fuel from freezing at temperatures as low as -15°C.

What is a possible effect of over-filling the engine with oil?
It could damage the catalytic converter.
BW0083R

Catalytic converters are part of most vehicles' exhaust system. They remove up to 75% of the carbon monoxide, nitrogen oxide and hydrocarbons from the vehicles' exhaust. Catalytic converters can be permanently damaged if, for example, the car is filled with leaded petrol rather than unleaded, or if the engine is over-filled with oil.

What should a driver do if the fuel system becomes air-locked?
Bleed the air out of the fuel system.
BW0084R

The fuel system can become air-locked if you let the fuel get too low or if there is a leak in the system. You should have the problem corrected before driving. The solution may be as simple as bleeding the fuel system to release the air.

Is a driver allowed to use rebated (green) diesel fuel in a car on a public road?
BW0085R

Green diesel may never be used in a car.

If, in its normal use, a vehicle is used on a public road, it must use unmarked (white) diesel, as the appropriate excise duties are included in the purchase price. You can be prosecuted for using green diesel in a vehicle on a public road.

Head restraints

What should a driver do to reduce the risk of neck injury in a rear-end collision?   BW0086R

Use a properly adjusted head restraint.

Head restraints are designed to protect the neck and spine in a collision and thus prevent or reduce whiplash. They should be properly adjusted for both the driver and the passengers.

Rear-view mirror on tractors

When must a tractor or works vehicle be fitted with a rear-view mirror?

A rear-view mirror must always be fitted.   BW0087R

All vehicles used on a public road must have a rear-view mirror to enable the driver to see road and traffic conditions behind and to each side.

Tyres

Your ability to control your vehicle, to steer it in the direction you want and to stop it when and where you want depends critically on the few square centimetres of rubber that are in contact with the road at any time. You must make sure that your tyres are in good condition and correctly inflated.

What is the minimum legal tread depth for tyres on cars?

1.6 millimetres   BW0088R

All road vehicles, except motorcycles and vintage vehicles, must have a minimum tyre tread depth of 1.6mm over the main tread. However, for safety reasons, you should replace the vehicle's tyres before they become this worn.

What does the load index of a tyre indicate?   BW0091

The maximum load a tyre can carry.

The load index indicates the maximum weight that a tyre can support safely. When replacing a tyre on your vehicle, you should make sure that the new tyre maintains the proper load index for the vehicle.

1

2

3

Under what circumstances could both cross-ply and radial tyres be fitted to a vehicle?   BW0092R
When each type is fitted on a different axle.

In general, you should fit the same type of tyres all round the vehicle. However if you need to fit a mix of cross-ply and radials, the tyres on any axle should be of the same type.

Clutch

What is the effect of resting the foot on the clutch pedal?   BW0093R
It wears out the clutch more quickly than normal.

The clutch is the connection between the engine and the gearbox. It enables the vehicle to move when a gear is engaged. When driving, you should not rest your foot on the clutch pedal, because it might disengage the selected gear and/or damage the clutch mechanism.

Side-impact protection bars

What is the purpose of side-impact protection bars?   BW0128
To protect the occupants when the vehicle is hit from the side.

Side-impact protection bars are fitted to some vehicles to protect the occupants of the vehicle in the event of a collision from the side.

Power-assisted steering

Power-assisted steering depends on a hydraulic system that includes a fluid reservoir. This reservoir should be kept filled in accordance with the manufacturer's instructions.

When the fluid reservoir is full to the mark, how would a driver check that the power-assisted steering is working effectively?   BW0094R
Turn the steering wheel from lock to lock with the engine running.

Before starting a journey, check that the PAS (power-assisted steering) is working by starting the engine and turning the steering wheel from full left lock to full right lock, to see that it operates smoothly and effectively.

What should the driver of a vehicle with power-assisted steering (PAS) do if steering becomes more difficult as they are driving?
BW0095R
Stop, check the level of the fluid and top up if necessary.

Most modern vehicles have power-assisted steering (PAS). PAS requires less effort and feels lighter, especially when carrying out manoeuvres such as parking, U-turns and reversing. You should be aware that it is easy to oversteer with PAS.

Seats

What is the effect of an incorrectly adjusted driver's seat?
BW0096R
It can delay the driver from operating a control.

Before starting a journey, you should adopt a suitable and comfortable driving position by adjusting the driver's seat to a position where all the vehicle controls can be operated efficiently.

Windscreen wipers and washer

You have to keep your windscreen clean and clear in order to see the road ahead and the traffic conditions around you, Your windscreen wipers and washer are essential pieces of equipment for this purpose, and you must know how to keep them in good condition.

While driving in rain, a driver notices that the wiper blades are worn. What should they do?
BW0097R
Have the blades replaced as soon as possible.

Use the windscreen wipers to keep the windscreen clear of rain, spray, snow or fog. Check them regularly to ensure that they are in good working order, and replace them when they become worn, before they become ineffective.

What should a driver do when the wiper blade on the driver's side is partly worn?
BW0103R
Have the worn blade replaced with a new one.

Use the windscreen wipers to keep the windscreen clear of rain, spray, snow or fog. Check them regularly to ensure that they are in good working order, and replace them when they become worn, before they become ineffective.

1
2
3

If the wiper blades are frozen to the windscreen, what should the driver do?

BW0098R

Defrost the windscreen before switching on the wipers.

Before starting a journey in icy weather, make sure that the windows are clear. Use the demister to clear the windows and defrost the wipers so that they can be used to clear the windscreen.

When a wiper blade fails to clear the windscreen what should the driver do?

BW0099R

Have the blades replaced as soon as possible.

Use the windscreen wipers to keep the windscreen clear of rain, spray, snow or fog. Check them regularly to ensure that they are in good working order, and replace them when they become worn, before they become ineffective.

What problem is indicated when wipers suddenly cease to function?

BW0100

A fuse has blown.

Check the vehicle's windscreen wipers regularly to ensure the blades are in good condition, and check that there is water in the washer bottle. If the wipers stop working suddenly, the most likely cause is a blown fuse.

What should a driver add to windscreen washer fluid in freezing weather?

BW0101R

A mild anti-freezing agent for windows.

In cold weather, use an anti-freezing agent in the windscreen washer fluid, so that the windscreen can be cleared if required.

Why is a windscreen laminated?

BW0104R

So as not to shatter into large fragments when struck by an object.

A laminated windscreen (a plastic film sandwiched between two layers of glass) is designed not to break into large fragments when struck by an object. This is to prevent serious injury to the driver and passengers.

What should a driver check regularly to ensure they have will have a good clear view of the road when driving? BW0105R

There is enough fluid in the windscreen washer reservoir.

Check the vehicle's windscreen wipers regularly to ensure the blades are in good condition, and check that there is water in the washer bottle.

What should a driver check regularly to ensure they have a good clear view of the road when driving? BW2

The windscreen wipers are working correctly.

Use the windscreen wipers to keep the windscreen clear of rain, spray, snow or fog. Check them regularly to ensure that they are in good working order, and replace them when they become worn, before they become ineffective.

Changing a wheel

The questions in this section check that you know how to change a wheel on a car safely.

When replacing a wheel, in what order should wheel nuts be tightened?

Tighten diagonally opposite nuts first. BW0111R

When fitting a wheel to your vehicle, tighten the nuts gradually and evenly by tightening them 'diagonally'. For example, if the wheel has four nuts, first tighten the two nuts along one diagonal, then tighten the nuts on the other diagonal. If the wheel has five nuts, tighten each alternate nut until all are tightened. All nuts should be tightened to the manufacturer's recommended torque.

When changing a wheel on their vehicle on a public road, what should a person do? BW0112

Turn on the hazard warning lights.

When changing a wheel on their vehicle on a public road drivers should make themselves as noticeable as possible by:
1. Wearing high visibility outer clothing
2. Putting the hazard warning lights on
3. Placing a red warning triangle to the rear of the vehicle on the right side or
4. A combination of all three actions

Environmental matters

Motor vehicles are a significant cause of pollution. In particular, they generate large amounts of the gases that are causing climate change. Other environmental effects include the amount of noise generated by engines and tyres.

All drivers should be aware of these effects, and modify their driving habits to minimise their negative impact on the environment. The questions in this section check that you understand the issues involved and that you know how to drive responsibly.

What should a driver do in order to avoid excessive exhaust pollution from their vehicle?

BW0107R

Have the vehicle's air filters changed regularly.

You should have your vehicle serviced regularly in accordance with the manufacturer's guidelines. A vehicle that is poorly tuned uses more fuel and creates more exhaust pollution. Air filters should be changed as part of normal servicing. If a vehicle is used in dusty conditions, the air filter may need to be changed more often. More information is available in the vehicle owner's handbook.

How regularly should a vehicle be serviced?

BW0108R

As often as indicated in the manufacturer's specification.

You should have your vehicle serviced regularly in accordance with the manufacturer's guidelines. This helps the vehicle to perform properly, thus saving fuel and reducing emissions. You should also carry out your own daily and weekly checks on fluid levels and tyres.

What is the purpose of a catalytic converter?

BW0109R

To reduce harmful exhaust emissions.

Catalytic converters are part of most vehicles' exhaust system. They remove up to 75% of the carbon monoxide, nitrogen oxide and hydrocarbons from the vehicles' exhaust.

What type of noise might fast cornering create?

BW0110

Tyre squeal.

If you drive around a corner too fast, the tyres begin to lose contact with the surface of the road, and this causes a squealing sound. If you continue driving in this way, you can lose control of the vehicle.

Getting out of the vehicle

Before you get out of your vehicle, check that opening the door will not interfere with other road users, and that you can get out safely. Similarly, when you are letting passengers out, you must make sure that they can do so safely.

What should a driver do before getting out of the vehicle? BW0113R
Check their side mirror and look behind before opening the door.

Before opening any door, check for other road users passing, and in particular look out for pedestrians, cyclists and motorcyclists. Exit the vehicle only when it is safe to do so, and close the door as soon as possible. Passengers should exit on the side nearest the kerb wherever possible.

How should a driver secure their vehicle before getting out of it? BW0114R
Apply the parking brake, stop the engine and engage a low gear.

Before leaving your vehicle, apply the handbrake, switch off the engine and engage a low gear. If the vehicle is fitted with automatic transmission, select 'P' (park).

What precaution should a driver take when getting out of their vehicle?
Check all around for approaching traffic and pedestrians before opening the door. BW0115

Before opening any door, check for other road users passing, and in particular look out for pedestrians, cyclists and motorcyclists. Exit the vehicle only when it is safe to do so, and close the door as soon as possible. Passengers should exit on the side nearest the kerb wherever possible.

On a busy road, how should a driver allow passengers out of a vehicle?
Stop and allow them to get out on the side nearest the kerb. BW0116R

Before allowing any door to be opened, check for other road users passing, and in particular look out for pedestrians, cyclists and motorcyclists. Passengers should exit on the side nearest the kerb, without getting in the way of pedestrians.

1
2
3

Which of the following checks should a driver perform on their vehicle before moving off?

RSA01046

Ensure that all doors are properly secured.

Before moving off it is advised to perform the 'Safety Checks' which includes the checking that all doors are safely closed.

What advice should a driver give to passengers before opening doors?

Check all around and open door with caution.

RSA01047

Before opening any doors, check for other road users nearby, inparticular motorcyclists and pedestrians.

How do you make sure your vehicle is parked safely?

RSA01048

Don't park it where it may endanger other road users.

When parking make sure you do not interfere with normal traffic flow and that your vehicle does not distrub, block or endanger other road users.

What should be considered when reversing out of a parking space?

Check for pedestrians and vehicles all around.

RSA01049

Some car parks are designed for you to park forwards to make it easier to load shopping. In these cases take extra care as you reverse out of the parking space because pedestrians and vehicles may pass behind you.

Seatbelts and child restraint systems

Any adult aged 17 years or over travelling in a car – whether in the front or the rear seat – is required to wear a seatbelt. Persons under the age of 17 who weigh more than 36 kg, or are more than 135 cm in height, must also wear adult seatbelts. Lighter, smaller children and babies must be restrained in special seats, harnesses or restraints. The questions in this section check that you know your responsibilities in this regard.

What cars are required to have rear seat belts fitted?
BW0117
Cars first registered after 1st January 1992.

Rear seat belts are compulsory on all cars registered after 1st January 1992.

Where seat belts are fitted to a car when must adult occupants wear them?
BW0118R
At all times.

The driver and all passengers in a car must wear a seatbelt or, in the case of a child, a suitable restraint system.

What is the purpose of a seat belt?
BW0119R
To prevent the wearer from being thrown forward in the event of a crash or abrupt deceleration.

Seatbelts save lives and reduce the risk of injury by restraining the occupants of a vehicle in the event of a crash or sudden deceleration.

When should a driver put on their safety belt?
BW0120R
Before they move off.

Before moving off, put on your seatbelt and make sure that all your passengers also have theirs on.

Who is responsible for ensuring that a passenger over 17 years of age is wearing a seat belt while travelling in a car?
BW0121R
The passenger only.

If the passenger is over the age of 17, it is their responsibility to comply with the seat belt regulations. Below that age, it is the driver's responsibility.

Who is responsible for ensuring that a passenger under 17 years of age is wearing a seat belt while travelling in a car?

BW0122R

The driver only.

If the passenger is over the age of 17, it is their responsibility to comply with the seat belt regulations. Below that age, it is the driver's responsibility.

In general, how should infants be secured in a vehicle?

BW0124

They should always be secured in a child restraint system.

As safety belts are designed mainly for adults and older children, infants and small children must be restrained in an appropriate child restraint system.

Should an infant who is not secured in a child restraint system be carried in the front passenger seat?

BW0125R

No, an infant must always be restrained in a correct child seat.

Infants and small children must be restrained in an appropriate child restraint system.

How should a child restraint system be secured in a vehicle?

BW0126R

It should be secured with seat belts or ISOFIX fittings.

A child restraint system should be secured in the vehicle either with the seatbelts of the car or with approved fixings. Always use a restraint system that is appropriate for the age, height and weight of the child, and follow the manufacturer's instructions.

What should a driver do when driving a vehicle with young children as passengers?

BW0127R

Make sure each child is wearing a seat belt or using an appropriate restraint system.

If the passenger is over the age of 17, it is their responsibility to comply with the seatbelt regulations. Below that age, it is the driver's responsibility.

Dealing with emergencies

The questions in this section deal with a number of emergency situations that you may find yourself in. They include getting a puncture while you are driving, skidding, breaking down, and avoiding a collision.

Punctures

A puncture is always an inconvenience, but it is also sometimes dangerous. If you get a sudden puncture while driving, you must know what to do in order to keep control of the vehicle and not endanger yourself or others.

What should a driver do if a tyre bursts on the vehicle they are driving?
Hold the steering wheel firmly and pull in on the side of the road.   BW0132R

If a tyre bursts on your vehicle, keep a firm hold of the steering, slow down gradually and stop where it is safe to do so. Switch on the hazard warning lights.

What should a driver do if they get a tyre blow-out on the road?
Apply the footbrake gently and bring the vehicle to a halt.   BW0140R

If a tyre on the vehicle you are driving blows out, slow down gradually and find a safe and suitable place to stop. Switch on your hazard warning lights and change the wheel or call for assistance.

What effect could a front-tyre blow-out have on a vehicle?
The steering wheel will pull to one side.   BW0141R

If a front tyre on the vehicle you are driving blows out, you will feel the effect of it through the steering wheel. The wheel will generally pull to the side of the blown-out tyre.

What effect could a rear-tyre blow-out have on a vehicle?
It could cause the vehicle to sway from side to side.   BW0142R

If a rear tyre on the vehicle you are driving blows out, the vehicle may sway from side to side, and this will affect its stability. Slow down, pull in where it is safe to do so, and switch on the hazard warning lights. Change the wheem or call for assistance.

1
2
3

Skidding

You should always drive in a way that is suited to the weather conditions and the state of the road. If you do, you will generally avoid skidding. However, if you do find yourself in a skid, you must know how to react in order to get the vehicle back into control as soon as possible. These questions check that you understand the causes of skidding and how to avoid them.

How should a driver use the brakes if the vehicle is fitted with anti-lock brakes (ABS)?
BW0135R

Press the brake pedal firmly and hold.

If your vehicle is fitted with ABS, brake firmly. ABS will not stop the vehicle more quickly, it will only prevent the wheels from locking. This helps you to maintain control of the vehicle.

What should a driver do if their vehicle gets into a four-wheel sideways skid?
BW0136R

Turn the steering wheel in the same direction as the skid and ease off the accelerator.

If your vehicle goes into a four-wheel skid, turn the steering wheel in the same direction as the skid and ease off the accelerator. This should help to bring the wheels back into line and allow you to regain control.

What should a driver do if their vehicle gets into a front-wheel sideways skid?
BW0137R

Release the accelerator.

If your vehicle goes into a front-wheel sideways skid, release the accelerator and do not try to steer until the tyres regain some grip on the road.

What should a driver do if their vehicle gets into a rear-wheel sideways skid?
BW0138R

Turn the steering wheel in the same direction as the rear wheels are heading.

If your vehicle goes into a rear-wheel sideways skid, turn the steering in the direction the rear wheels are heading. This should be done very gradually, as too much steering could cause the vehicle to skid in the opposite direction.

How should a driver in a vehicle without anti-lock brakes (ABS) deal with a front-wheel straight-line skid?
BW0139R

Press and release the footbrake at rapid intervals.

If your vehicle does not have ABS and it goes into a straight-line front-wheel skid due to braking, press and release the brake pedal repeatedly and rapidly. This will help to restore tyre grip and enable you to regain control.

Breakdowns and emergencies

If your vehicle breaks down, you should make sure that it does not cause a hazard to other road users, and that any action you take does not put you or others in danger. You must also know how to react and respond to emergency situations, and how to bring your vehicle to a stop quickly and safely.

What action should a driver take if the engine in their vehicle cuts out suddenly when they are driving along?
BW0143R

Signal and steer the vehicle to the side of the road.

If the engine in the vehicle you are driving cuts out, signal and steer to the side of the road. Switch on the hazard warning lights and contact the relevant breakdown service to get assistance.

How would hydraulic power steering be affected if an engine stalled in slow-moving traffic?
BW0144R

The steering would become heavy and difficult to operate.

Hydraulic power steering is operated by a pump which is driven by the engine. If the engine stalls, the pump stops working, and the steering becomes heavy and requires much more effort to turn.

When driving on the road, what should a driver do if the brakes on their vehicle fail?
BW0145R

Engage a lower gear.

If the brakes on the vehicle you are driving fade or fail, select a lower gear to slow the vehicle down and move to the left to come to a halt.

When driving on the road, what should a driver do if the brakes on their vehicle fail?
BW0146R

Pump the brake pedal rapidly.

If the brakes on the vehicle you are driving fail, try to regain some braking by pumping the footbrake. This may help you to bring the vehicle to a safe stop.

What should a driver do if the accelerator jams when they are driving along?
BW0147R

Engage neutral gear and apply the brakes.

If the accelerator on the vehicle you are driving jams, select neutral and use the brakes to bring the vehicle to a safe halt. Switch off the engine as soon as the vehicle has stopped. Get the vehicle checked out before attempting to drive again.

When driving along, a driver feels that the oncoming car may crash into their vehicle. What should they do?
BW0148R

Flash the headlights and sound the horn to attract the attention of the other driver.

If there is an oncoming vehicle in your path, flash your lights and sound your horn to alert the other driver. Bring your vehicle to a halt immediately.

When driving along and confronted by an obstacle, what should a driver do?
BW0149R

Apply the footbrake firmly.

To stop your vehicle in an emergency, apply the footbrake firmly, and maintain the pressure until the vehicle stops. Depress the clutch pedal just before stopping.

When driving along and required to stop suddenly, what should a driver do?
BW0150R

Apply the footbrake firmly.

To stop your vehicle in an emergency, apply the footbrake firmly, and maintain the pressure until the vehicle stops. Depress the clutch pedal just before stopping.

When required to stop in an emergency, what should a driver do?
Maintain firm pressure on the footbrake.   BW0151R

To stop your vehicle in an emergency, apply the footbrake firmly, and maintain the pressure until the vehicle stops. Depress the clutch pedal just before stopping.

When required to stop in an emergency, what should a driver do?
Press the footbrake firmly.   BW0152R

To stop your vehicle in an emergency, apply the footbrake firmly, and maintain the pressure until the vehicle stops. Depress the clutch pedal just before stopping.

What should a driver do to avoid having to make an emergency stop?
Keep a safe distance from the vehicle in front.   BW0153

When driving in traffic, read the road ahead and keep a safe distance from the vehicle in front. Use the two-second rule to determine your safe distance from the vehicle in front.

When changing a wheel on their vehicle on a public road what should a person do?
                      BW3
Place a red warning triangle to the right side at the rear of the vehicle.

When changing a wheel on a public road, make yourself as visible as possible. Wear high-visibility outer clothing, turn on the hazard warning lights, and place a red warning triangle to the rear of the vehicle on the right-hand side.

When changing a wheel on their vehicle on a public road what should a person do?
                      BW4
Wear reflective clothing if available.

When changing a wheel on a public road, make yourself as visible as possible. Wear high-visibility outer clothing, turn on the hazard warning lights, and place a red warning triangle to the rear of the vehicle on the right-hand side.

What should a driver do to avoid having to make an emergency stop?
Scan the road well ahead.   BW5

When driving in traffic, read the road ahead and keep a safe distance from the vehicle in front. Use the two-second rule to determine your safe distance from the vehicle in front.

Safety issues of particular importance for motorcyclists

1
2
3

Before you ride a motorcycle, you must be well prepared. You must equip yourself with the appropriate protective clothing, and you must be thoroughly familiar with the features and controls on the bike you are riding.

Protection and clothing

The questions in this section relate to the ways in which you can protect yourself from injury in the event of a fall or other incident. Some of them relate to legal requirements and some to recommended good practice.

What should someone always wear while riding a motorcycle? AM0001R
Gloves, boots, helmet and protective clothing.

You should always wear appropriate clothing and a secure helmet when riding a motorcycle, on every journey, no matter how short. Motorcycle gloves, boots, helmets and protective clothing are designed to protect the wearer from adverse weather conditions and against injury in the event of a crash or fall.

What standard should a motorcyclist's protective clothing meet? AM0002R
A standard certified by a CE mark, that is European Union Standards Mark.

You should always wear appropriate clothing and a secure helmet when riding a motorcycle, on every journey, no matter how short. Jackets and trousers should be designed to protect you from impact and abrasion as well as from adverse weather conditions. Motorcycle clothing that claims to give protection must be marked with a European Standard CE Mark. You should wear a reflective jacket to make you more visible to other road users.

When should a motorcyclist wear protective clothing? AM0003R
In all situations.

You should always wear appropriate clothing and a secure helmet when riding a motorcycle, on every journey, no matter how short. Protective clothing is designed to protect you from adverse weather conditions and to help protect you from injury in the event of a crash or fall.

What footwear should a motorcyclist wear while riding? AM0004R
Protective boots.

You should wear secure and reinforced boots on every journey. Shoes, sandals or runners do not offer any protection from the weather or support in the event of a crash or fall. Boots should be high enough to protect your shins and support your ankles.

1
2
3

Why should someone wear gloves when riding a motorcycle?   AM0005R
To protect the motorcyclist's hands in the event of a fall.

You should wear proper motorcycle gloves on every journey. These will protect your hands from the wind and rain, and help you to avoid injury in the event of a crash or fall. Choose gloves that offer maximum protection without hindering your ability to operate the controls easily.

Under what circumstances should a motorcyclist wear gloves?   AM0006R
At all times.

You should wear proper motorcycle gloves on every journey. These will protect your hands from the wind and rain, and help you to avoid injury in the event of a crash or fall. Choose gloves that offer maximum protection without hindering your ability to operate the controls easily.

How should a motorcyclist protect their eyes when riding a motorcycle?
By wearing a helmet with an adjustable visor.   AM0007R

You should always wear appropriate eye protection. Most helmets have an adjustable visor to protect the eyes from wind, rain, stone chippings, flies and insects. If the helmet does not have a visor, you should wear goggles.

When is it permitted to ride a motorcycle or moped on a public road, without wearing a helmet?   AM0008R
Never.

You are legally required to wear a proper helmet while riding a moped or motorcycle in a public place. The helmet should meet EU standards and be securely fastened. It is illegal to wear an unsecured helmet, and an unsecured helmet is unlikely to be effective in the event of a crash.

Motorcycle features, taking care of the machine, safety

Modern motorcycles are complex machines. Before you take one onto the public road, you need to be totally familiar with all its features and controls, and know how to use them.

What does this light mean when displayed on the instrument panel?

AM0009R

The motorcycle is in neutral gear.

You should know and understand the various warning lights on the instrument panel. This green light tells you that neutral gear is engaged. It is important to know this before starting the engine.

What does this switch operate?

AM0010R

Headlight.

This switch is used to alternate between dipped beam and main beam when riding at night. Motorcyclists should always travel with dipped headlight during the day.

On a motorcycle with manual transmission, what does this lever operate?

AM0011R

The clutch.

On a modern motorcycle with manual transmission, this lever is used to operate the clutch. It is used to disengage the drive between the engine and the driven wheel when moving away, stopping and changing gears.

What does this switch operate?

AM0012R

The emergency engine stop.

This switch operates the emergency engine stop or 'kill' switch. It should not normally be used to stop the engine except in emergency situations, such as after a crash or fall. However you should check it periodically to make sure that it is operating properly.

1
2
3

What does this lever operate?
AM0013R

The front brake.

On a modern motorcycle, this lever is used to operate the front brake. To apply the brake, you squeeze the lever. The harder you squeeze, the more pronounced is the braking effect. As the front brake is the most effective brake on the motorcycle, it should be used with care and precision when slowing or stopping.

Which fluid is contained in this reservoir?
Brake fluid.
AM0014R

Modern motorcycles fitted with hydraulic brakes normally have the front brake fluid reservoir mounted on the right-side handlebar. The reservoir can be either a clear container or one with a sight-glass to enable the fluid level to be checked. You should check this regularly with the motorcycle in an upright position on a level surface.

What does this foot lever, located on the nearside of a modern motorcycle, operate?
The gears.
AM0015R

On a modern motorcycle, the gear lever is located on the nearside (left side) just in front of the footrest. You select gears by lifting or pushing down the lever with your foot. You should familiarise yourself with your own motorcycle, as the number of gears varies with make and model.

What does this foot lever, located on the offside of a modern motorcycle, operate?
The footbrake.
AM0016R

On a modern motorcycle fitted with manual transmission, the rear brake lever is located on the offside (right side) in front of the footrest. You apply the rear brake by pressing the pedal with your foot. The rear brake is not as effective as the front, so you should use it in conjunction with the front brake for optimum stopping power.

What does this light mean when displayed on the instrument panel?
AM0017R

A gear is not engaged.

You should know and understand the various warning lights on the instrument panel. This green light tells you that a gear is not engaged. It is important to know this before starting your engine.

What action should a motorcyclist take in the event of a front-wheel sideways skid?
AM0018R

Steer in the same direction that the motorcycle is heading and release the throttle.

In the event of a sideways skid, you should steer the motorcycle in the direction of the skid. Skids can be avoided by adjusting your speed to suit the road and traffic conditions.

What on a motorcycle should be checked weekly?
AM0019R

Petrol, oil, water, damage, electrics and tyres.

You should carry out a routine check on your motorcycle weekly. Checks should include petrol, oil, water, damage, electrics and rubber (tyres). If the bike is chain-driven, you should also check and lubricate the chain.

How should a motorcyclist take care of their motorcycle?
AM0020R

Visually inspect the motorcycle daily and carry out an inspection once a week.

A motorcycle in regular use should be checked daily, with a more detailed inspection once a week. Depending on the season and the usage of the motorcycle, these maintenance intervals may vary.

What should a motorcyclist check before starting the engine?
AM0021R

That neutral gear is selected.

You should know and understand the various warning lights on the instrument panel. The green light tells you that neutral gear is engaged. It is important to know this before starting the engine.

1
2
3

What is likely to happen if a motorcyclist fails to lubricate the drive chain on their motorcycle?
AM0022R

The rate of chain wear will increase.

You should inspect, lubricate and adjust your drive chain regularly, depending on your usage of the bike. Failure to lubricate the chain properly will increase the rate of wear dramatically. Special lubricants are available specifically for this purpose.

What could happen if the drive chain on a motorcycle is loose?
AM0023R

The rear wheel could lock.

If a motorcycle chain is worn or loose, it could come off its sprockets and cause the rear wheel to lock, with a resultant loss of control.

What might happen if a motorcycle is ridden while the drive chain is slack?
AM0024R

The rear wheel might lock.

If a motorcycle chain is worn or loose, it could come off its sprockets and cause the rear wheel to lock, with a resultant loss of control.

What might happen if the drive chain of a motorcycle is incorrectly adjusted?
AM0025R

It could cause a rattling noise.

It is important for the chain to be in good working condition. If a motorcycle chain is worn, loose or badly adjusted, it will generally create a rattling noise, and this should prompt you to investigate and address the problem.

What could happen if a motorcycle is ridden with a worn drive chain?
The chain may stretch and become more noisy.
AM0026R

If a motorcycle chain is worn or loose, it could come off its sprockets and cause the rear wheel to lock, with a resultant loss of control. A worn chain will generally create a rattling noise, and this should prompt you to investigate and address the problem.

What should be checked after the drive chain has been adjusted?
Wheel alignment.   AM0027R

When you adjust the drive chain, you should make sure that the rear wheel is properly aligned.
Otherwise the tyre may wear prematurely and the handling of the bike will be affected,
especially during cornering.

What is the effect of applying the choke for a long period?
Increased fuel consumption and pollution.   AM0028R

The engine runs on a mixture of fuel and air. When the engine is cold, you should apply the
choke to increase the amount of fuel in the mix. However, if you leave the choke on for a long
time, it will lead to an increase in fuel consumption and pollution.

What could happen if the choke is left on?
Engine wear and fuel consumption could increase.   AM0029R

The engine runs on a mixture of fuel and air. When the engine is cold, you should apply the
choke to increase the amount of fuel in the mix. However, if you leave the choke on for longer
than necessary, engine wear and fuel consumption will increase.

What should a motorcyclist be aware of concerning cable-operated brakes?
AM0030R
That they stretch in use.

Cable-operated brakes should be inspected regularly to check that they are operating
effectively. If the cable is frayed, it should be replaced, and if the brakes are not effective
enough, the cable may need to be tightened.

In the interest of road safety, what should be kept clean on a motorcycle?
AM0031R
Headlight.

Motorcyclists are responsible for keeping their motorcycles in good condition. Keeping the
lights (front and rear), reflectors and number plate clean will increase your visibility to other
road users.

In the interest of road safety, what should be kept clean on a motorcycle?
AM0032R

Rear lights.

Motorcyclists are responsible for keeping their motorcycles in good condition. Keeping the lights (front and rear), reflectors and number plate clean will increase your visibility to other road users.

What is a possible effect of incorrect wheel alignment on a motorcycle?
Reduced road holding.
AM0033R

If the wheels are incorrectly aligned, the bike will run out of line. This will affect the handling and road holding of the bike, especially when cornering.

What is a possible cause of a badly aligned rear wheel?
AM0034R

Refitting the rear wheel.

When refitting a rear wheel to a motorcycle, you should make sure that it is aligned precisely behind the front wheel. Failure to do so could result in uneven tyre wear and/or instability when cornering.

What could happen if the steering head bearings are worn on a motorcycle?
AM0035R

The motorcycle could be difficult to control.

The steering head bearings provide for smooth steering on a motorcycle. If they are worn, the steering becomes loose or wobbly, and the motorcycle becomes unstable.

What would cause the steering to feel wobbly?
AM0036R

Worn steering head bearings.

The steering head bearings provide for smooth steering on a motorcycle. If they are worn, the steering becomes loose or wobbly, and the motorcycle becomes unstable. The bearings should be adjusted or replaced if necessary to restore smooth precise steering.

Under what circumstances should the engine cut-out switch be used?
In an emergency only.   AM0037R

You should use the engine cut-off switch only in an emergency, such as after a crash or a fall. However you should check it periodically to make sure that it is operating properly.

Why should a motorcyclist ensure the side stand is fully raised before moving away?   AM0038R
To avoid catching the ground and destabilising the motorcycle when cornering.

Use the side stand only for parking the motorcycle. Raise it fully before moving away. Riding with the side stand down is dangerous, as it may dig into the ground when cornering and cause you to lose control of the bike.

When should tyre pressures be increased?   AM0040R
When carrying a pillion passenger.

You may need to increase the tyre pressures on a motorcycle when carrying extra weight, such as a pillion passenger and / or luggage. Consult your owner's manual for the relevant tyre pressures.

What is the minimum legal tyre tread depth for motorcycles?   AM0041R
1.0 millimetres.

The minimum tyre tread depth for motorcycles is 1mm. However, it is advisable to replace the tyre before it wears that low to improve road holding, especially in wet weather. Some tyres have a wear indicator in the groove to show that the tyre is getting near to the minimum legal requirement.

What does the traction control system help to prevent?   AM0043R
Wheelspin when accelerating.

A traction control system on a motorcycle helps to prevent wheelspin when accelerating. This helps you to maximise the grip of the rear tyre when accelerating in slippery conditions, both when moving away and on bends and corners.

1
2
3

What is the effect of applying the choke for a long period?
The engine may run too fast.   AM1

If you leave the choke on for longer than necessary, the idle speed of the engine will increase, which could make it more difficult to control the bike at lower speeds or when slowing or stopping.

In the interest of road safety, what should be kept clean on a motorcycle?   AM2
Number plate.

Motorcyclists are responsible for keeping their motorcycles in good condition. Keeping the lights (front and rear), reflectors and number plate clean will increase your visibility to other road users.

What is a possible effect of incorrect wheel alignment on a motorcycle?
Excessive tyre wear.   AM3

If the wheels are incorrectly aligned, the bike will run out of line. This will result in excessive or uneven tyre wear.

Riding your motorcycle

The questions in this section relate to the basic skills that you need
to ride a motorcycle – starting and stopping the bike, moving off,
adopting the appropriate position on the road, overtaking safely, taking
emergency and corrective action and dealing with hazards.

1

2

3

Moving off

Moving off requires very fine control of the clutch lever, throttle and rear brake. Avoid jerky or sudden movements of the controls so that you don't jerk forward or cut out (stall). You also need to let each of your feet take your weight at different times. The questions below check that you understand these matters.

What should a motorcyclist check before starting the engine?   AM0044R
That the gear selector is in neutral.

Before starting the engine, you should ensure that the gear selector is in neutral. This can be verified by checking that the green neutral light is showing on the instrument panel.

A motorcyclist in busy moving traffic wishes to change lanes. Why is a 'lifesaver look' required?   AM0045R
The mirror may not cover blind spots.

A 'lifesaver look' is a last look to the left, right or the rear into the blind spot areas not covered by the mirrors. You should give a lifesaver look before moving off and before changing direction.

What should a motorcyclist do just before moving off from a parked position?   AM0046R
Look over their shoulder for a final glance.

The final glance before moving away from the kerb is known as a 'lifesaver look'. A lifesaver look is a final look to the left, right or rear into the blind spot areas not covered by the mirrors. You should give a lifesaver look before moving off and before changing direction.

What is a 'lifesaver look'?   AM0047R
A look over the shoulder just before moving off, turning or changing lanes.

A 'lifesaver look' is a last look to the left, right or the rear into the blind spot area not covered by the mirrors. You should give a lifesaver look before moving off and before changing lanes or direction.

When should a motorcyclist perform a 'lifesaver look'?   AM0048R
Before changing direction on a motorcycle.

A 'lifesaver look' is a last look to the left, right or the rear into the blind spot area not covered by the mirrors. You should give a lifesaver look before moving off and before changing direction.

Road position

For your own safety and the safety of other road users, it is important that you adopt the correct position on the road. Where lanes are not marked, you should keep to left, but not too close to the verge or to parked cars or the pavement. If the road is wet, you should avoid splashing pedestrians and cyclists. Where lanes are marked, you should adopt a position centrally between the lane markers. If you are going to turn off to the left or right, plan ahead, so that you are in the correct lane when you arrive at the junction.

In what position should a motorcyclist have their feet when stopped at traffic lights, Stop signs or in traffic?   AM0054R
The left foot down.

When stopped in traffic, you should have your left foot down to balance and your right foot on the rear brake to secure the motorcycle.

In what position should a motorcyclist have their feet when driving along in traffic?   AM0055R
Both feet up.

In order to maintain proper balance and control, you should always keep your feet on the foot rests while the motorcycle is in motion.

In this traffic situation, what is the position of the motorcyclist?   AM0059R
In the correct position.

The motorcyclist is in the correct position for the traffic situation. When travelling on a single carriageway road with two-way traffic, the correct position is halfway between the centre of the road and the left-hand side. However you should also consider the width of the road, the road surface, and any obstructions when riding.

Under what circumstances should a motorcyclist take a 'life saver' look?
Before changing lane.   AM24

A 'life saver' look is a look over the left or right shoulder to observe the blind spot area which is not covered by the mirrors. This should be done before you move off, before you change your position on the road, and before you make a U-turn.

On a single-track country road, what should a motorcyclist do? AM0060R
Avoid the grass in the centre of the road.

When you are riding on a single-track country road, you should avoid the grass and debris that collects down the centre of the road, as this may cause instability and result in a fall.

In normal riding, what is the correct position on the road? AM0070R
Mid-way between the near side and the centre of the road.

The normal position is in the centre of the lane. On a single carriageway road with two-way traffic, the correct position is half-way between the centre of the road and the left-hand side. However, you should also take the width of the road, the condition of the road surface and any obstructions into consideration when riding.

What position should a motorcyclist take up behind a vehicle they are about to overtake? AM0072R
The off-side of the vehicle in front.

When you intend to overtake the vehicle in front, you should position your bike to the off-side rear of the vehicle in front, leaving enough room to get a good view of the road ahead. You can then take the opportunity to overtake smoothly and safely.

When and why should a motorcyclist take up a near-side position? AM0073R
When approaching a right-hand bend, to get an early view of the road ahead.

When approaching a right-hand bend, you may take up a position towards the left of the lane, so as to gain a better view of the road ahead. This generally would apply outside of special speed limit areas.

When should a motorcyclist take up a near-side position? AM0074R
In good time before turning left.

Before turning left, you should take up the near-side (left-hand side) position. This prevents other traffic from passing on your inside and enables following traffic to continue ahead or to turn right in safety.

When riding in wet weather, what in particular should a motorcyclist be aware of?
AM0075R

That oil or diesel may gather on parts of the road.

When riding in wet weather, you should watch out for oil and/or diesel spillages. These can be identified by a rainbow-coloured film on the road. Avoid such areas if possible, as they are particularly dangerous for motorcyclists.

What is the main advantage of riding in the central position, midway between the near-side edge and the centre line of the road?
AM0076R

It gives the rider a good margin of safety on each side.

The normal position when riding on a single carriageway road with two-way traffic is half-way between the centre of the road and the left-hand side. The advantage of riding in this position is that you are more visible to other traffic, and you are in a better position to avoid potholes and road debris. It also reduces the potential for conflict with oncoming traffic.

What is the advantage of taking up an off-side position?
AM0077R

To get an early view through a left-hand bend.

When approaching a left-hand bend, you may position yourself towards the right of the lane, to give you a better view of the road ahead. This generally would apply outside of special speed limit areas.

Under what circumstances should a motorcyclist take up an off-side position?
AM0078R

In good time before turning right.

Before turning right, you should take up an off-side (right-side) position. This makes you more visible to other road users and allows following traffic to pass on your inside.

When a motorcyclist is cornering, what should they do?
AM0079R

Lean in the direction of the turn.

When you are cornering, you should lean towards the inside of the bend or curve. In this position, the force of gravity works to keep the bike stable. If you do not lean the bike into the curve or bend, its tendency is to continue in a straight line.

1
2
3

What effect does cornering at speed have on a motorcycle? AM0080R
The motorcycle is less stable.

Cornering at speed reduces the stability of the bike and places extra demands on tyre grip. These effects increase with the severity of the bend, and the speed and weight of the bike.

On approach to a right-hand bend with a restricted view ahead, what position should a motorcyclist adopt? AM0081R
The near-side position.

When approaching a right-hand bend with a restricted view of the road ahead, you should take up a position towards the left (near side) of the road, so as to gain a better view of the road ahead. This generally would apply outside of special speed limit areas.

How should a motorcyclist approach a bend? AM0082R
At the correct speed.

When approaching a bend, you should take up the correct position on the road, adjust your speed and select the appropriate gear for that speed. Going through the bend, you should maintain your line and a constant speed, in order to ensure stability and maximum tyre grip. This is especially important on a road that is uneven or wet.

What should a motorcyclist ensure during cornering? AM0083R
That the speed is correct.

When cornering, you should maintain a correct and constant speed to ensure stability and maximum tyre grip. This is especially important on a road that is uneven or wet.

What should a motorcyclist allow for when negotiating a bend? AM0084R
A change to poor road conditions.

When cornering, you should expect the unexpected. A change in road conditions, such as potholes or mud on the road, or the emergence of other traffic from an exit, could lead to an incident.

What should a motorcyclist allow for when negotiating a bend? AM7
Blind junctions or exits.

When cornering, you should expect the unexpected. A change in road conditions, such as potholes or mud on the road, or the emergence of other traffic from an exit, could lead to an incident.

What is the advantage of correct positioning while cornering? AM0085R
It gives an earlier and more extended view of the road ahead.

The advantage of taking up the correct position while cornering is that it gives you an early view of the road ahead through the bend. On left-hand bends it offers increased safety margins from hazards at the side of the road, and on right-hand bends it offers increased safety margins from oncoming traffic.

What position should a motorcyclist take up on approach to a left-hand bend? AM0086R
The off-side position.

The off-side position gives a better view of the road ahead past a left-hand bend. You should, however, be aware of the possibility that oncoming vehicles may be straddling the centre of the road, in which case you should move more to the left.

What should a motorcyclist consider before taking up position on a left-hand bend? AM0087R
Whether or not oncoming traffic requires a margin of safety.

When approaching a left-hand bend, you should consider whether taking up the off-side position is necessary. For example, if oncoming vehicles are close to the centre of the road, it might be better to maintain the central position or a near-side position.

When riding in an urban area, what should a motorcyclist consider before taking up position on a left-hand bend? AM0088R
Whether their position on the road might mislead other traffic into thinking that they intend to turn right.

Before taking up an off-side position on a bend in an urban area, you should be sure that your position will not mislead other road users. If following traffic believes that you are about to turn right, they may attempt to overtake you on your inside.

1

2

3

What effect does cornering at speed have on a motorcycle?

In correct position.

Extra demands are placed on tyre grip.

AM4

Cornering at speed reduces the stability of the bike and places extra demands on tyre grip. These effects increase with the severity of the bend, and the speed and weight of the bike.

How should a motorcyclist approach a bend?

In the correct position.

AM5

When approaching a bend, you should take up the correct position on the road, adjust your speed and select the appropriate gear for that speed. Going through the bend, you should maintain your line and a constant speed, in order to ensure stability and maximum tyre grip. This is especially important on a road that is uneven or wet.

How should a motorcyclist approach a bend?

In the correct gear.

AM6

When approaching a bend, you should take up the correct position on the road, adjust your speed and select the appropriate gear for that speed. Going through the bend, you should maintain your line and a constant speed, in order to ensure stability and maximum tyre grip. This is especially important on a road that is uneven or wet.

How should a motorcyclist gauge the severity of a bend?

AM0089R

By noting where the near-side and off-side verges appear to meet and how this changes on approach.

Most bends and corners are marked with yellow warning signs. As you enter the bend, take note of the point at which the near-side verge and the off-side verge appear to meet, and note how this point changes as you proceed through the bend. This allows you to gauge the severity of the bend and adjust your speed as required.

Why is special care required when taking bends on a motorcycle with a sidecar attached? AM0090R

The sidecar compartment cannot be leaned over.

Special care is needed when riding a motorcycle with a sidecar attached. This is particularly the case on bends and when turning – you cannot lean the unit in the way you can with a solo motorcycle, and the unit needs to be steered with a deliberate push or pull on the handlebars. This requires considerably more effort than leaning.

Why is special care required when taking a left-hand bend on a motorcycle with a sidecar attached? AM0091R

The weight being thrown outwards will tend to lift the sidecar off the road.

Special care is needed when riding a motorcycle with a sidecar attached, especially when taking a left-hand bend, as the weight being thrown outwards tends to lift the sidecar off the road

---

What should a motorcyclist consider before taking up position on a left-hand bend? AM8

Whether it is really necessary to alter course if their view ahead is unrestricted.

When approaching a left-hand bend, you should consider whether taking up the off-side position is necessary. If there is an unrestricted view of the road ahead, it may be better to maintain your central position while going through the bend.

1
2
3

Overtaking

The ability to overtake slower-moving vehicles safely is one you need to develop. You should always be extremely careful when overtaking on the open road and should always ask yourself these questions: Is it necessary? Is it legal? and Is it safe? Remember that on a bike you are not as visible to other road users as larger vehicles, such as cars, trucks and buses.

What should a motorcyclist avoid when overtaking?   AM0092R
Causing oncoming traffic to alter course or speed.

Before overtaking another vehicle, you should make sure that the road ahead is clear and that you can overtake safely without causing oncoming traffic or the traffic being overtaken to alter their speed or course. You should also allow sufficient clearance to the traffic being overtaken in case they alter course during the manoeuvre.

What should a motorcyclist avoid when overtaking on a single   AM0093R
carriageway road with two-way traffic?
Making a third line of vehicles abreast.

When you are overtaking another vehicle on a single carriageway road with two-way traffic, you must not make a third lane abreast either by overtaking a vehicle that is itself already overtaking or by overtaking a vehicle when there is oncoming traffic, even if you do not cross the centre line of the road.

A motorcyclist is travelling in a near-side position behind a truck and wishes to take up an off-side position. What should they be aware of?
That areas of the road ahead will be lost from view while they are changing position.   AM0097R

If, while following a large vehicle, you change from a near-side position to an off-side position, your view of the road ahead will be greatly reduced while you are making the change, and your ability to see bends and other hazards will be reduced.

When overtaking a slow-moving truck, what hazard might arise?   AM0098R
The truck might turn right with late or no signal.

When you are preparing to overtake a slow-moving truck or large vehicle, there are many things to be aware of as a motorcyclist. You need to be aware not only of the vehicle ahead but also of other situations that may develop. Other road users may do something unexpected and may not always be as aware as they should be of a rider's presence.

Having just overtaken a large vehicle on a dual carriageway or motorway what should a motorcyclist do before moving back into the left-hand lane?   AM0099R
Check the left-hand mirror, signal and move back when it is safe to do so.

After overtaking a large vehicle, you should check your left-hand mirror, signal, give a lifesaver look to the left and gradually move back into the left-hand lane without cutting across the vehicle you have overtaken.

A motorcyclist has moved closer to the vehicle in front prior to overtaking it. What should they be most aware of?   AM0100R
The driver in front may brake suddenly.

As you approach the vehicle in front prior to overtaking it, you should be aware that you will have less time to react if the driver in front accelerates, slows or brakes suddenly. You should therefore assess all the hazards on the road ahead before taking up this position, and if the overtaking opportunity does not arise you should fall back to a safe following distance.

What should a motorcyclist avoid when overtaking?
Causing traffic being overtaken to alter course or speed.   AM9

Before overtaking another vehicle, you should make sure that the road ahead is clear and that you can overtake safely without causing oncoming traffic or the traffic being overtaken to alter their speed or course. You should also allow sufficient clearance to the traffic being overtaken in case they alter course during the manoeuvre.

What should a motorcyclist avoid when overtaking?   AM10
Being unable to move back to the near side in plenty of time.

When you are overtaking another vehicle, you should make sure that you can return to your own side of the road in plenty of time.

1
2
3

When overtaking a slow-moving truck, what hazard might arise? AM11
A slow-moving vehicle might be turning left onto the road up ahead.

When you are preparing to overtake a slow-moving truck or large vehicle, there are many things to be aware of as a motorcyclist. You need to be aware not only of the vehicle ahead but also of other situations that may develop. Other road users may do something unexpected and may not always be as aware as they should be of a rider's presence.

When overtaking a slow-moving truck, what hazard might arise? AM12
The driver of a vehicle on a road to your left up ahead is turning right and is unaware of your presence.

When you are preparing to overtake a slow-moving truck or large vehicle, there are many things to be aware of as a motorcyclist. You need to be aware not only of the vehicle ahead but also of other situations that may develop. Other road users may do something unexpected and may not always be as aware as they should be of a rider's presence.

When overtaking a slow-moving truck, what hazard might arise? AM13
The driver of a vehicle turning left from a junction on the right up ahead might have taken observations only to their right.

When you are preparing to overtake a slow-moving truck or large vehicle, there are many things to be aware of as a motorcyclist. You need to be aware not only of the vehicle ahead but also of other situations that may develop. Other road users may do something unexpected and may not always be as aware as they should be of a rider's presence.

A motorcyclist has moved closer to the vehicle in front prior to overtaking it. What should they be most aware of? AM14
The driver in front may reduce speed.

As you approach the vehicle in front prior to overtaking it, you should be aware that you will have less time to react if the driver in front accelerates, slows or brakes suddenly. You should therefore assess all the hazards on the road ahead before taking up this position, and if the overtaking opportunity does not arise you should fall back to a safe following distance.

A motorcyclist has moved closer to the vehicle in front prior to overtaking it. What should they be most aware of? AM15
The driver in front may accelerate suddenly.

As you approach the vehicle in front prior to overtaking it, you should be aware that you will have less time to react if the driver in front accelerates, slows or brakes suddenly. You should therefore assess all the hazards on the road ahead before taking up this position, and if the overtaking opportunity does not arise you should fall back to a safe following distance.

Taking emergency/corrective action

When riding a bike, you need to always expect the unexpected. You literally don't know what's around the next bend, but you can avoid some dangerous situations by developing your observation skills and learning to anticipate danger. Even the best and safest motorcyclists, however, will have to make emergency stops from time to time. The quicker you respond to a potential emergency, the more likely you are to avert it. So, keep alert and be ready.

What should a motorcyclist do if they get a sudden and severe puncture while riding?

AM0101R

Close the throttle and ease to a stop.

If you get a sudden and severe puncture while riding along, you should not brake suddenly as this would cause the bike to become more unstable. You should hold the handlebars firmly, ease off the throttle, and gradually bring the bike to a safe stop at the side of the road.

How should a motorcyclist normally stop their engine?

AM0102R

Turn off the ignition.

The normal sequence in stopping a motorcycle engine is as follows: Close the throttle. Engage neutral. Switch off the engine using the ignition key. Switch off the fuel tap (if fitted). If you use the ignition key to stop the engine, you are less likely to leave the key in the ignition when leaving the motorcycle. The emergency engine stop switch should be used only in an emergency.

How should a motorcyclist apply the brakes to stop quickly in an emergency?

AM0103R

Use the front brake followed by the rear brake.

When braking in an emergency, you should close the throttle and apply the front brake just before the rear, and increase the brake pressure steadily. You should consider the road and weather conditions, and apply the right amount of braking to each wheel to achieve maximum effort without causing the wheels to lock up and skid.

What should a motorcyclist do if their motorcycle engine cuts out while they are riding along?
AM0104R

Signal and steer the motorcycle to the side of the road.

If you are riding along and your motorcycle engine cuts out, you should check behind, signal and steer to the side of the road as soon as possible.

What action should a motorcyclist take in the event of a front-wheel sideways skid?
AM0105R

Turn the steering in the same direction as the motorcycle is heading and roll off the throttle.

In the event of a sideways skid, you should steer the bike in the direction of the skid. You should release the throttle or the brake, whichever is causing the skid. You can avoid skidding by adjusting your speed to suit the road, weather and traffic conditions.

What action should a motorcyclist take in the event of a rear-wheel sideways skid?
AM0106R

Turn the steering in the same direction as the rear wheel is heading and roll off the throttle.

In the event of a sideways skid, you should steer the bike in the direction of the skid. You should release the throttle or the brake, whichever is causing the skid. You can avoid skidding by adjusting your speed to suit the road, weather and traffic conditions.

Dealing with hazards

A hazard is anything that means you might have to change the position, speed, or direction of your motorcycle. For example, a road feature such as a sharp bend could be a hazard, and so could the actions of other road users.

As you become more experienced as a motorcyclist and build up experience of road and traffic conditions, you will become better at scanning the road ahead to anticipate and react to the different kinds of hazard that you meet. This will help you to further develop the essential skills of observation, judgement, planning and reaction.

What should a motorcyclist do when meeting a large vehicle on a narrow road? AM0107R

Slow down and proceed with caution.

If you meet a large vehicle on a narrow road, you should slow down and move to the left, provided it is safe to do so. You should also be prepared for other vehicles that may be hidden behind the approaching vehicle.

What should a motorcyclist be aware of when meeting a large vehicle on a narrow road? AM0108R

Forward visibility is reduced.

If you meet a large vehicle on a narrow road, you should slow down and move to the left, provided it is safe to do so. You should also be prepared for other vehicles that may be hidden behind the approaching vehicle.

What hazard should a motorcyclist be aware of in this situation? AM0110R

Wet road surface.

You should exercise caution when travelling on wet roads. Allow extra time for slowing or stopping, as tyre grip will be reduced. Take extra care when braking or cornering on wet surfaces.

In this situation, what does the motorcyclist need to consider? AM0114R

They might be blown off course by wind turbulence from the oncoming truck.

When riding in the off-side position, you should be aware of any oncoming vehicles, especially those travelling near or over the centre of the road. You should also be prepared for wind turbulence created by large vehicles coming towards you at high speed.

What should a motorcyclist be aware of on approaching a railway crossing? AM0115R

The tracks may not be flush with the road.

Approach railway crossings with caution. Reduce speed and be prepared to stop if necessary. Be prepared for changes in the road surface. The tracks might not be at the same level as the road. Be aware also that the tracks and any road markings may be slippery in wet conditions.

What should a motorcyclist be aware of on approaching a railway crossing? AM16

The barrier may come down.

Approach railway crossings with caution. Reduce speed and be prepared to stop if necessary. Be prepared for changes in the road surface. The tracks might not be at the same level as the road. Be aware also that the tracks and any road markings may be slippery in wet conditions.

Weather conditions

On a motorcycle, you are much more exposed to the weather than drivers of cars or trucks, and you are much more likely to be destabilised or put off course by bad weather. Any kind of weather that makes it more difficult for you to see what's happening on the road (and makes it more difficult for other road users to see you) presents particular riding challenges, especially while you are learning. Rain, fog, snow, ice, high winds, and even bright sunshine can present hazards that you must be prepared for. The questions in this section deal with your ability to meet these challenges.

What should a motorcyclist do while riding through a flood?   AM0117R
Keep the engine running fast.

Approach flooded areas with caution. If the flood water seems too deep, consider an alternative route. If it is not too deep, ride through in a low gear and keep the engine running fast in order to prevent water entering the exhaust.

1

Having gone through floods, how would a motorcyclist dry the brakes?
Drive slowly while applying the brakes briefly.   AM0118R

After riding through a flooded area, test your brakes immediately. The brakes can be dried by gently applying them a few times until normal braking is restored.

2

3

What should a motorcyclist be aware of when there is melting tar on the road?   AM0119R
Melting tar reduces tyre grip.

In very hot weather, tarmac road surfaces can become soft. When this happens, you should take extra care when braking and cornering, as tyre grip will be reduced.

In hot weather what can be made worse by soft tar on the road? AM0120R
Braking.

In very hot weather, tarmac road surfaces can become soft. When this happens, you should take extra care when braking and cornering, as tyre grip will be reduced.

What should motorcyclists do when riding in windy conditions? AM0121R
Look ahead and anticipate crosswinds.

in strong winds, you can become more vulnerable on a motorcycle. Slow down and try to anticipate where crosswinds are most likely to affect you, such as when passing gaps in roadside hedges or between tall buildings, or on exposed roads and high bridges or flyovers. Be aware that the winds might also affect other road users, such as pedestrians, cyclists and high-sided vehicles.

How would a motorcyclist know if there was black ice on the road?
Tyre noise will decrease. AM0122R

Black ice occurs when moisture freezes on a very cold surface. Exposed roads and bridges can have black ice when other sections of the same road may be clear. Black ice is virtually invisible, and so presents a particular hazard for motorcyclists. In wintry conditions, if you notice a reduction in tyre noise or if the steering becomes lighter, you should suspect that there may be black ice on the road.

What in particular should a motorcyclist be aware of when travelling in hot weather and the tar on the road is melting and soft? AM25
Stopping distances are increased.

In very hot weather, tarmac road surfaces can become soft. When this happens, you should take extra care when braking and cornering, as tyre grip will be reduced.

Keeping your distance

At all times, you must make sure to stay a safe distance from the vehicle in front of you, and be satisfied that you can stop within the distance that you can see to be clear.

What is the advantage to a motorcyclist of staying well back from the vehicle in front while riding? AM0125R
It gives the rider a safe braking distance.

In good weather, you should maintain at least a two-second gap from the vehicle in front, and more in poor conditions. This gap gives you sufficient room to brake safely in the event that the vehicle in front slows or changes direction suddenly. It also allows you to see the road in front of the vehicle ahead.

What is the advantage to a motorcyclist of staying well back from the vehicle in front while riding? AM0126R
It gives the rider a safe braking distance.

In good weather, you should maintain at least a two-second gap from the vehicle in front, and more in poor conditions. This gap gives you sufficient room to brake safely in the event that the vehicle in front slows or changes direction suddenly. It also allows you to see the road in front of the vehicle ahead.

What should a motorcyclist be aware of when following close behind a larger vehicle? AM0127R
They will be in the blind spot of the driver of the vehicle in front.

If you ride too close behind a large vehicle, the driver of that vehicle may not be aware that you are there. You will also be hidden from the view of oncoming traffic.

What should a motorcyclist do if they are following a vehicle on a wet road and an overtaking vehicle pulls into the gap between them and the vehicle in front? AM0128R
Ease back to regain a safe distance.

When in traffic on a wet road, you should allow at least a four-second gap between you and the vehicle in front. If another vehicle overtakes you and pulls into this gap, you should slow down and restore the four-second gap between you and the vehicle in front.

What should a motorcyclist be aware of when following close behind a larger vehicle?
AM18

Their visibility to oncoming traffic will be reduced.

If you ride too close behind a large vehicle, the driver of that vehicle may not be aware that you are there. You will also be hidden from the view of oncoming traffic.

Which of these has an effect on stopping distance?
Tyre condition.
AM19

Worn or improperly inflated tyres reduce the grip of your tyres on the road, with the result that your motorcycle may skid during an emergency stop.

Which of these has an effect on stopping distance?
Road conditions.
AM20

Road surfaces that are wet, icy or loose reduce tyre grip, and extend your stopping distance considerably. At 80km/h on a good dry road, stopping distance is typically 53 metres, whereas on a wet road this increases to 81 metres.

Braking and stopping

While you are learning to ride, one of the most important skills you need to master is how to slow down, brake and bring your bike to a stop. Your bike has front and rear brakes and you need to learn how to use them individually and together.

When should the rear brake of a motorcycle be used on its own?
During slow manoeuvres.   AM0129R

Under normal circumstances, you should apply the front brake just before the rear brake. The front brake is considerably more powerful than the rear. However when travelling at very slow speeds, using the rear brake alone can result in smoother control.

When should a motorcyclist avoid using the front brake?   AM0130R
When the motorcycle is banked over, turning or on a loose surface.

Avoid using the front brake while banked over in bends, while turning at a junction, and on loose surfaces. Using the front brake in these situations can cause the motorcycle to straighten up in the road and go straight on, or cause the loss of tyre grip, leading to a skid. If you must brake on a bend, use the rear brake.

What should a rider avoid doing when a motorcycle is banked over?
Using the front brake.   AM0131R

Avoid using the front brake while banked over in bends, while turning at a junction, and on loose surfaces. Using the front brake in these situations can cause the motorcycle to straighten up in the road and go straight on, or cause the loss of tyre grip, leading to a skid. If you must brake on a bend, use the rear brake.

What should a motorcyclist do when descending a long steep hill?
Engage a lower gear at an early stage.   AM0132R

When descending a long steep hill, you should use engine braking to maintain a steady speed. Changing down a gear or two increases the effect of the engine braking. This reduces wear on the brakes, and helps ensure that they do not overheat and that they are more effective when needed.

1
2
3

What should a motorcyclist do when descending a steep and winding road? AM0133R

Use the brakes on the straight only.

It is always safer to brake when travelling upright in a straight line. On a steep and winding road, you should use a combination of engine braking and the normal brakes as necessary on approaching the bends. Braking in a bend can cause the bike to straighten up and go straight on, or to a loss of tyre grip leading to a skid.

When should a motorcyclist brake firmly? AM0134R

Only when travelling in a straight line.

It is always safer to brake when travelling upright in a straight line. You should avoid braking on bends, and always adjust your braking to suit the road conditions.

When should a motorcyclist brake firmly? AM0135R

Only on the straight.

It is always safer to brake when travelling upright in a straight line. You should avoid braking on bends, and always adjust your braking to suit the road conditions.

How should a motorcyclist apply both brakes? AM0136R

Apply the front brake followed by the rear.

To stop safely in good weather and road conditions, you should apply the front brake followed by the rear. More pressure should be applied to the front, as this gives the best stopping power. In wet conditions, equal pressure should be applied to both brakes.

How should braking force be distributed when stopping a motorcycle on a straight road in dry conditions? AM0137R

Apply slightly more pressure to the front.

To stop safely in good weather and road conditions, you should apply the front brake followed by the rear. More pressure should be applied to the front, as this gives the best stopping power. In wet conditions, equal pressure should be applied to both brakes.

How should braking force be distributed when stopping a motorcycle on a straight road in wet or slippery conditions?
AM0138R

Apply the same amount of pressure to both brakes.

In wet or slippery conditions, you should apply equal pressure to front and rear brakes.

Which of these has an effect on stopping distance?
AM0139R

The speed of the motorcycle.

Speed affects the stopping distance of a motorcycle. At 50km/h in dry conditions, stopping distance is typically 24 metres, whereas at 100km/h this increases to 78 metres.

What effect has a sidecar on the stopping distance of a motorcycle?
It increases stopping distance, especially going downhill.
AM0140R

The extra weight of the sidecar increases the stopping distance, especially going downhill.

What is the stopping distance of a vehicle travelling at 80km/h on a good dry road?
AM0141R

53 metres.

When travelling at 80km/h in good dry conditions, stopping distance is approximately 53 metres. This is made up of 15m reaction distance and 38 metres braking distance.

Which of these has an effect on stopping distance?
AM0143R

Reaction time.

Stopping distance is the sum of reaction distance and braking distance. An alert and fit rider takes between half a second and one-and-a-quarter seconds to react. In this time, a motorcycle travelling at 80km/h will travel about 15 metres before the brakes are even applied. Reaction time can be negatively affected by age, alcohol, drugs, fatigue, state of health and mental condition.

1
2
3

Stability and skidding

The most common cause of a skid is going too fast for the road conditions, or jerky braking, gear changing or steering. You can reduce the likelihood of skidding by riding smoothly at an appropriate speed, and by keeping your distance from the vehicle in front. Be particularly careful when approaching bends, especially those on a downslope. Don't rely on your ABS to prevent you from skidding – it won't always do so.

What might cause a rider to lose control of a motorcycle? AM0144R
Water on the road.

You are more likely to skid or lose control of your motorcycle in bad weather conditions, when road surfaces tend to be more slippery. You should be on the alert for wet surfaces, mud or gravel, and wet leaves on the road. These conditions will be more hazardous near bends or at junctions where you will need to brake, accelerate or change direction.

What effect could crossing tram tracks at an oblique angle have on a motorcycle? AM0145R
It could destabilise the motorcycle.

You should cross train or tram tracks with caution, especially when they are at an oblique angle to your path. The road surface may be uneven. The tracks may not be at the same level as the road, and your motorcycle may lose stability while crossing the tracks.

What can happen if a rider applies both brakes, with greatest pressure on the rear? AM0149R
The rear wheel may lock.

When you apply the brakes on the motorcycle, your weight and that of the motorcycle shift forward onto the front wheel, and the weight on the rear wheel is reduced. If you apply too much braking force to the rear wheel at this stage, it may lock up, causing a skid. Under normal conditions, you should apply the front brake first, followed by the rear, with the greater pressure on the front

1

2

3

What should a motorcyclist do if the throttle sticks open while they are riding alone?
AM0150R

Operate the engine cut-out switch.

In an emergency situation, such as the throttle sticking open, you should use the 'kill' switch (emergency engine stop) to stop the engine and bring the motorcycle safely to a halt. This switch may also be used to stop the engine after a collision or a fall.

What is a possible effect of riding over road markings such as lines and directional arrows?
AM0151R

Tyre grip may be reduced, particularly in wet weather.

The paint used in the road markings can be slippery, especially in wet weather. You should try to avoid riding over these markings where possible.

What in particular should a motorcyclist be aware of when crossing tram tracks?
AM0152R

The tracks may be slippery, particularly when wet.

You should approach tram and railway crossings with caution. The road markings and tracks can be slippery, especially in wet weather. You should also look out for broken road surfaces on these crossings.

1
2
3

What would be the result of excessive use of mirrors?

Ability to read the road ahead would be impaired.
AM0154R

You should read the road ahead and react accordingly. Using the mirrors excessively or looking behind excessively will distract your main focus from the road in front and may extend your reaction time.

What can a motorcyclist do to reduce the risk of skidding?

Accelerate gently.
AM0155R

Excessive acceleration can cause the front wheel of your motorcycle to lift from the road or cause the rear wheel to spin. Each of these causes a loss of stability and may lead to the motorcycle going out of control or skidding. Always use gentle acceleration and ride within your own limits.

What action can a motorcyclist take to avoid skidding?
AM0157R

Avoid using the front brake when the motorcycle is banked over.

As motorcycles have less tyre contact on the road than other vehicles, you should always brake in a controlled manner. Avoid using the front brake when the machine is banked over in order to reduce the risk of skidding.

What action should a motorcyclist take if the rear wheel skids under acceleration on wet surfaces?
AM0159R

Ease off the throttle.

Take care when accelerating in wet conditions. Too much acceleration can cause the rear wheel to skid, with the risk that you will lose control of the bike. If the rear wheel does start to skid, ease off the throttle to reduce the power going to the rear wheel.

What might cause a rider to lose control of a motorcycle?
Wet leaves on the road.
AM21

You are more likely to skid or lose control of your motorcycle in bad weather conditions, when road surfaces tend to be more slippery. You should be on the alert for wet surfaces, mud or gravel, and wet leaves on the road. These conditions will be more hazardous near bends or at junctions where you will need to brake, accelerate or change direction.

What might cause a rider to lose control of a motorcycle?
Mud on the road.
AM22

You are more likely to skid or lose control of your motorcycle in bad weather conditions, when road surfaces tend to be more slippery. You should be on the alert for wet surfaces, mud or gravel, and wet leaves on the road. These conditions will be more hazardous near bends or at junctions where you will need to brake, accelerate or change direction.

Alert driving and consideration for other road users

You need to be fully alert when you are riding a motorcycle, so don't ride when you are very tired. Tiredness is a factor in many road collisions.

You should also behave with consideration and courtesy towards other road users, including pedestrians, cyclists, motorists and drivers of larger vehicles.

How other drivers see you

As a motorcycle rider, you must constantly bear in mind that you are not as visible to other road users as, for example, cars, trucks or buses. You must try to make sure that you avoid situations that put your own life or that of other road users in danger.

What in particular should a motorcyclist be aware of when approaching a junction from which a vehicle is emerging? AM0160R

The driver of the emerging vehicle may underestimate the motorcyclist's speed.

Junctions are particularly hazardous for motorcyclists. Many drivers do not take proper observations when emerging from a side road, and fail to notice a motorcyclist. You should bear this in mind when approaching junctions with side roads.

What in particular should a motorcyclist be aware of when approaching a side road? AM23

Drivers of emerging vehicles may not see the motorcyclist.

As a vulnerable road user a motorcyclist should pay particular attention when approaching side roads as the drivers of emerging vehicles may not have seen them. If in doubt slow down and try to make eye contact with the driver. You should always ride defensively and be prepared to stop if necessary.

1
2
3

What in particular should a motorcyclist be aware of when travelling on a dual carriageway? AM0161R

Other vehicles may change lane without checking their blind spots.

When you are travelling on a dual carriageway, you should read the road ahead and be prepared for the possibility that other traffic may change lane without making proper observations or giving adequate warning.

What in particular should a motorcyclist be aware of when following a large truck or bus? AM0162R

Vehicles emerging from side roads may not see the motorcycle behind the larger vehicle.

When you are on a motorcycle following behind a large truck or bus, you will not be easily visible to motorists emerging from side roads. Always read the road ahead and allow plenty of space between your motorcycle and the vehicle in front.

In general, how can a motorcyclist make other road users more aware of their presence on the road? AM0164R

Avoid travelling in other vehicles' blind spots.

You should always try to make other road users aware of your presence on the road. Where possible, avoid travelling in other road users' blind spots.

In general, how can a motorcyclist make other road users more aware of their presence on the road? AM0165R

By riding in a position where they can be seen and keeping a good distance from other traffic.

You should always try to make other road users aware of your presence on the road. Where possible, ride in a position in which you can be seen by other drivers. Avoid riding too close to the vehicle in front.

See and be seen

High hedges and the winding nature of country roads can impair visibility – blind corners, sharp bends and dips in the road can be particularly dangerous. You should always adjust your speed to suit the road you are driving on and you must never exceed the speed limit. In many cases, a safe speed might be much less than the stated speed limit for the road. You need to be able to stop the bike in the road space that you can see – if you can't, you're going too fast.

You should also make sure that other road users can see you.

What should a motorcyclist do to improve their ability to see in very heavy rain? AM0166R

Reduce speed.

In heavy rain, reduce speed. This gives you more time to see and react to changes in road and traffic conditions.

What should a motorcyclist do to improve their visibility to other road users? AM0167R

Wear reflective or fluorescent material.

Motorcyclists are less visible to other road users, so they need to increase their visibility by wearing bright or reflective clothing and by riding with their dipped headlamp on.

What should a motorcyclist do to improve their visibility to other road users? AM0168R

Drive with a dipped headlight on.

Motorcyclists are less visible to other road users, so they need to increase their visibility by wearing bright or reflective clothing and by riding with their dipped headlight on.

Under what circumstances should a motorcyclist take a 'life saver' look?

Before making a U-Turn. AM0170R

A 'life saver' look is a look over the left or right shoulder to observe the blind spot area which is not covered by the mirrors. This should be done before you move off, before you change your position on the road, and before you make a U-turn.

1
2
3

What should a motorcyclist do before making a U-Turn? AM0171R
Take a 'life saver' look and check the road is clear in both directions.

Before making a U-turn a motorcyclist should always take the appropriate observations to the rear, including a 'life saver' look. A 'life saver' look is a look over the left or right shoulder to observe the blind spot area which is not covered by the mirrors.

Under what circumstances should a motorcyclist take a 'life saver' look to check for other traffic? AM0172R
Before changing direction.

A 'life saver' look is a look over the left or right shoulder to observe the blind spot area which is not covered by the mirrors. This should be done before you move off, before you change your position on the road, and before you make a U-turn.

When riding a motorcycle around a bend on an unlit road at night with no oncoming traffic, which light should a motorcyclist use? AM0174R
Full beam headlight.

On an unlit road at night, you should use your main beam headlight to help you see and be seen. However, use dipped headlights when there is approaching traffic or pedestrians on the road.

Under what circumstances should a motorcyclist use full high-beam headlights? AM0175R
When riding on unlit roads at night.

Use full high-beam headlight when riding on unlit roads at night. When you have the full beam light on, a blue warning light is shown on the instrument panel.

What should a motorcyclist do when travelling on a main road with traffic emerging from side roads who may not see the motorcycle? AM0176R
Look well ahead and read the road.

When you are travelling along a road that has many junctions with emerging traffic, try to read the road ahead and be prepared to react and respond to any vehicle turning into your path. Always adjust your speed to suit the road and traffic conditions.

When riding on a main road, a motorcyclist sees a vehicle emerging from a side road into their path. What action should the rider take? AM0177R
Slow down and be ready to stop.

Try to read the road ahead and be prepared to react and respond to any vehicle turning into your path. Be ready to slow down or stop if necessary.

How can riding a more powerful motorcycle change the rider's attitude?
The motorcyclist may have the impression that they are travelling slower than they actually are. AM0178R

Powerful motorbikes tend to be quiet, produce little vibration and go fast without straining the engine. On such a bike, you might gain speed without realising it and find yourself in a situation that you cannot control.

What should a motorcyclist do before changing lanes from left to right?
Mirror, indicate and give 'life saver' look to the right. AM0179R

You should check your mirrors, indicate and give a 'life saver' look to the right to make sure that it is safe to change lane.

Bad roads, bad weather and bad times of day

As a motorcyclist, you are particularly vulnerable on uneven road surfaces, in bad weather and in poor lighting conditions. You must learn to deal with these hazards by adjusting your style of driving, and particularly by lowering your speed so that you can react safely and in good time to any changes in road or traffic conditions.

What lights must be shown by a motorcyclist at night? AM0180R
Headlight, red rear light, number-plate light and red rear reflector.

On a moped or motorcycle, you are legally required to have a headlight, a red rear light, a number plate light and a red rear reflector. These should be checked regularly and kept clean. This will help to ensure that you can be seen at night.

1
2
3

What lights should a motorcycle show when parked at night on an unlit road?

A white light to the front and a red light to the rear. AM0181R

If a motorcycle is parked on an unlit road at night, it creates a potential danger for other road users. It is the rider's responsibility to ensure that their motorcycle can be seen, so they must switch on their vehicle's parking lights (white to the front and red to the rear). On most motorcycles, this can be done by turning the key another click past the 'lock' position on the ignition switch, after which the key can be removed.

How can strong winds affect a motorcyclist? AM0182

They can blow the motorcyclist off course.

A sudden gust of wind can blow a motorcyclist off course, especially in cross winds. Take extra care in windy conditions, as there is a danger that you will be blown into the path of other vehicles.

What should a motorcyclist do when travelling in fog? AM0183R

Slow down, use dipped headlight and keep to the centre of the driving lane.

When travelling in fog, use your dipped headlight and maintain a position in the centre of your lane. Drive with extreme caution and be prepared to react and respond to changes in road or traffic conditions.

What in particular should a motorcyclist be aware of when travelling in hot weather and the tar on the road is melting and soft? AM0184R

The road may be slippery.

In very hot weather, tarmac road surfaces can become soft. When this happens, you should take extra care when braking and cornering, as tyre grip will be reduced.

Bright sunlight can make it difficult for other road users to see what?

The indicators on a motorcycle. AM0185R

In bright sunlight, a motorcycle's brake lights and indicators might not be clearly seen. In such circumstances, you should consider giving a clear hand signal to inform other road users of your intentions.

Scope of the m[...]
and learner perm[...]

The questions in this section deal with [...]
categories of motorcycle driving licence [...]

Under what circumstances may th[...] carry a pillion passenger?
Never.

It is against the law for the holder of a motorcycl[...] at any time.

What is the maximum engine capacity o[...] ...otorcycle that the holder of a category A1 driving licence may ride?
AM0187R
125cc.

The holder of a category A1 driving licence is restricted to riding motorcycles of 125cc or less, with a power rating of 11kw or less.

What is the maximum engine power of a motorcycle that may be ridden by a person holding a category A1 licence?
AM0194
11 kilowatts.

A category A1 driving licence limits the holder to riding motorcycles with a maximum engine power output of 11 kilowatts.

What is the minimum engine capacity that a motorcycle must have in order to travel on a motorway?
AM0204
50cc

To travel on a motorway, a motorcycle must have an engine capacity of 50cc or more and be capable of travelling at least 50 km/h.

mainly with carrying pillion passengers legally and safely.

umstances may a child be allowed to ride a motorcycle in e?

AM0195R

e minimum age at which a motorcycle can be ridden in a public place is 16. A motorcycle learner permit cannot be issued to anyone under this age.

How should a motorcyclist maintain their balance while carrying a passenger on the motorcycle?

AM0196R

Instruct the passenger to lean over on bends in the same direction as the rider.

In order to maintain proper balance and control of your motorcycle when carrying a passenger, you should advise the passenger to lean the same way as you do when travelling around bends.

How should a motorcyclist maintain their balance while carrying a passenger on the motorcycle?

AM0197R

Instruct the passenger to lean over on bends in the same direction as the rider.

In order to maintain proper balance and control of your motorcycle when carrying a passenger, you should advise the passenger to lean the same way as you do when travelling around bends.

Under what circumstances is a passenger allowed to sit sideways on a motorcycle?

AM0199

Never.

Passengers should always sit on a motorcycle facing forward with both feet on the footrests.

Environmental impact of motorcycling

The motor industry is making substantial efforts to reduce the environmental damage caused by driving. Modern cars and motorcycles are generally much more efficient in their use of fuel, have lower greenhouse gas emissions, and cause less pollution.

As individual motorcyclists, we can also do quite a lot to reduce our personal carbon footprint and to minimise the impact our road use has on the environment.

What would be the effect of taking the exhaust off a motorcycle?
Noise and smoke pollution would increase.   AM0200

The exhaust is fitted to an engine to control noise and smoke pollution. If it is removed, noise and smoke pollution is increased. The performance of the engine is also affected.

Which of the following is the environmentally friendly way to dispose of motorcycle waste engine oil?   RSA01013
Bring it to a specialist waste disposal facility.

Waste engine oil is regarded as hazardous waste and you should only disposed of it by bringing it to a specialist waste disposable facility where it will be disposed of in an environmentally friendly manner.

Getting off the motorcycle

In general, you should get off the bike on the left side – this means that you will be on the side away from other traffic. When dismounting, pay attention to the difference in level between the road and the kerb, and be careful of slippery underfoot surfaces – such as loose gravel.

What should a motorcyclist do before getting off a motorcycle?
Look behind to make sure it is safe.   AM0201

You should always look behind before getting off a motorcycle. In general, you should get off on the left-hand side, away from traffic.

What should a motorcyclist do before a passenger gets off the motorcycle? AM0203

Look behind to make sure it is safe.

You should always look behind before allowing a passenger to get off your motorcycle. The passenger should get off on the left-hand side, away from traffic.

What should a motorcyclist do after overtaking a large vehicle on a dual-carriageway? AM0205

Check the left-hand mirror, signal, and move in to the left when it is safe to do so.

When you have overtaken a larger vehicle, you should check your mirror and signal, then make sure that it is safe to move back in to the left and that you have left sufficient room for the larger vehicle.

Why should a motorcyclist dismount a motorcycle from the left side?

Because that side is usually away from traffic passing. RSA01012

For your own safety you should always dismount from a motorcycle on the left side as that is the side away from passing traffic.

Who is responsible for ensuring a pillion passenger is wearing a properly fitted crash helmet when traveling on a motorcycle? RSA01014

The rider.

It is the responsibility of the rider to make certain the passenger is wearing a properly fitted crash helmet.

Turns: go wide (opposite side of lane
of turn direction)